Teaching and Dramatizing Greek Myths

Teaching and Dramatizing Greek Myths

Josephine Davidson

Illustrated
by
Fiona Starr

1989
TEACHER IDEAS PRESS
A Division of
Libraries Unlimited, Inc.
Englewood, Colorado

TEACHER IDEAS PRESS
A Division of Libraries Unlimited, Inc.
P.O. Box 3988
Englewood, Colorado 80155-3988

Library of Congress Cataloging-in-Publication Data

Davidson, Josephine.
    Teaching and dramatizing Greek myths / by Josephine Davidson ;
illustrated by Fiona Starr.
    xiv, 263 p. 22x28 cm.
    Includes bibliographical references.
    ISBN 0-87287-735-3
    1. Mythology, Greek--Juvenile drama.   2. Mythology, Greek--Study
and teaching (Secondary)   I. Title.
PS3554.A9256T4   1989
812'.54--dc20   89-36699
                                                                    CIP

To My Sister

Gina

Contents

Five Love Stories

Introduction

Teaching and Dramatizing Greek Myths is for junior high teachers who want to inspire their students with a love for mythology. It is also for those who want to use the classics in the teaching of reading, writing, and speaking skills. It is designed to help you turn your class into a joyful learning experience by dramatizing the myths. Supporting eight of the plays in the book are teachers' notes, vocabularies, activities, tests, games, and puzzles. The final five plays, the *Love Stories*, leave the development of this supporting material up to the teacher.

Mythology offers an escape from reality, an experience in which one can stretch the imagination and at the same time deal with the everyday reality of reading, writing, and speaking skills. Students at the junior high level are just beginning to grow independent. They have a real need to identify with other young people, to know that other young people, even those thousands of years ago, faced similar problems. And they need to be *doing*. They find it impossible to sit through lectures and long reading sessions. Mythology is a subject most young people like and plays keep them *doing* rather than just reading and listening. Although I wrote these plays with junior high students in mind, many of them have been successfully presented by fifth and sixth graders.

I wrote the first play, the *Odyssey*, out of desperation. A ninth grade class I was teaching showed a decided lack of interest in the assigned translation. The class was hampered by unfamiliar terminology. I searched catalogs looking for plays and material to supplement this tedious reading. Nothing was available. I had the inspiration to skip some chapters and start with the action, the actual voyage of Odysseus. Next came puppet construction for in-class staging, and the students were caught up in the creativity. At home I wrote the play keeping one act ahead of the students who were taping the play during the class period. Later we went back and read the rest of the *Odyssey*. Four years later a student was asked by a reporter to name her outstanding memory of high school. She quickly answered, "The Odyssey."

As a junior high teacher for twenty-three years, I came to realize that it is important for a student at junior high level to have a thorough grounding in mythology. Upon entering high school the student will then be prepared to read and appreciate not only the *Iliad* and the *Odyssey*, but also Shakespearean plays and other literature with mythological allusions. Without a foundation in mythology students are lacking tools needed for this more sophisticated reading.

In writing these plays I took the basic plots from mythology. Sometimes I combined two or three versions of a particular myth in order to come up with a more substantive plot. However, the dialogue is my own. It is impossible to be definitive about locations, activities, monsters, or people in mythology. The stories, having been told and retold for centuries, have many different versions and interpretations. (The Gray Sisters, for example, were reported to have lived in three different places in three different stories.) If it seemed an important enough point, the apparent contradictions in the stories have been pointed out in the teachers' notes. Because spelling of mythological references varies from source to source, I have attempted to use the most widely accepted American spellings.

These plays were written with puppet performances in mind so there are never more than six characters on stage at a time. However, the plays are easily adapted to the stage with any number of students added as extras. The puppet theater takes up limited space and can be folded when not in use. The puppet show involves all of the class, giving the students opportunities to use organizational, artistic, and musical abilities. Taping the dialogue gives tight control over timing allowing the teacher to know exactly how long a performance will take.

The teachers' notes are to help the teacher plan each presentation. Map transparencies are to acquaint the students with the area they will be reading about. Vocabulary words and definitions are listed just after the teachers' notes. Discussion worksheets include questions formulated using Bloom's taxonomy. The last question on each worksheet is either a research or writing request and can be assigned for homework.

The Test Yourself Worksheet is a review aid. The MYTHO game is a bingo game designed as a culmination activity. Since the MYTHO game needs fifty questions some plays were not long enough to provide fifty questions, hence not each play has a MYTHO game. The crossword puzzles, using mythological clues, can be an additional culmination activity.

Mythology enhances many subjects. The student can study astronomy, finding the constellations and matching them with their mythological names. The student learns basic map skills using Greece and the Mediterranean as the focal point in geography. The English assignments include writing about characters and events and enlarging the topic sentences by example, comparison, contrast, and chronology. The students will improve their speaking skills by participating in plays, extemporaneous myth telling, and making oral reports. With the assistance of the physical education teacher, the students can organize Olympic games on the original Greek model.

Mythology is a high-interest subject for students of junior high age if approached creatively. Since students this age find it difficult to concentrate for long periods of time, participating in reading and producing plays is a happy solution. Not all the plays need to be produced. Read through the plays, having students do all the assignments and then pick out the play to be produced. As an alternative the class can be divided into groups and each group allowed to produce its own play, possibly one of the shorter Love Stories.

Without certain people this book would not have come to life. My special thanks to Virginia Shea and M. Xavier McPhee, of Santa Rosa, California who were never too busy to answer my questions, or research material for me. And cheers for Dan Davis of Houston, Texas, for his practical advice. I am especially grateful to Fiona Starr, a Bellingham, Washington, high school senior who not only did the illustrations but proofread the manuscript several times and read the plays aloud with me. Thank you to my husband, Peter, for all his technical help, including the puppet theater drawings and most of all for his support.

THE PLAY

Cast of Characters
In Order of Appearance

Odysseus, king of Ithaca
Man #1, crewman
Man #2, crewman
Polyphemus, a Cyclops
Elpenor, very young crewman
Eurylochus, crewman who is a nobleman
Hermes, messenger of the gods
Circe, witch
Man #3, crewman
Teiresias, blind prophet
Mother of Odysseus, ghost
Zeus, king of the gods
Athena, goddess of wisdom
Calypso, enchantress
Nausicaa, young daughter of Alcinous
Queen Arete, mother of Nausicaa
King Alcinous, king of Phaeacians
Two men and one woman of the court

Act I. Odysseus meets the Cyclops.

SCENE 1. Ship's deck.

[curtain]

Odysseus, center stage, sits with his head in his hands. After twenty seconds, he slowly lifts his head.

Odysseus: I am Odysseus, son of Laertes of Ithaca. [stands and walks to front of stage and addresses the audience] Ithaca is a harsh land but I know of no other sight, other than one's own country, that brings such tears of joy. I have for ten years been trying to reach my homeland. [pause] But it is a long tale … [Odysseus back up to center stage and is joined by Eurylochus, Elpenor, and Man #1 and Man #2, who enter from the left.]

Eurylochus: [anxiously] Royal master, I plead with you. Let us not sink our anchor in this water. Rather, we should make haste now before the sun sets. We have had such terrible experiences on strange lands.

Odysseus: Men, we must not dwell on the past. It is true that the Ciconians nearly ruined us and we were well rewarded to escape with our lives. The joy of our escape, however, is saddened by the knowledge that we lost so many men.

Eurylochus: Then, I beg you Odysseus, let us get out of this harbor. Remember the last time we sent a few men to explore the land of the Lotus-eaters? They ate the lotus and forgot all about us. It is better if we do not set foot on this strange land.

Elpenor: I am so young. Please, let us sail quickly away from here.

Odysseus: [momentarily putting arm around Elpenor's shoulder] You forget that we need supplies. This land is luxuriant. The water is so beautifully clear as it cascades down to the sea. We can easily beach our boats. This harbor is so protected that we do not need to tie up. Come men.

Eurylochus: You go, Odysseus. Leave me here with most of the men.

Odysseus: I find it hard to deal with you, Eurylochus, you of noble birth, but I will do as you suggest. [to audience] Eurylochus is my brother-in-law. Yes, he is married to my sister and this close relationship gets in the way sometimes. [to crewmen] Come on men, follow me. [exits]

[curtain]

SCENE 2. Inside cave.

[curtain]

Enter Odysseus, followed by Man #1 and Man #2.

Odysseus: Look at the cheeses!

Man #1: See the fresh fruit!

Man #2: And see the pails for fresh milk. And the lambs! O, mighty feast! I am so hungry I will indulge myself right now.

Odysseus: No, friends, do not eat anything. We must await our host. Somebody is coming now.

[Polyphemus enters from right]

Polyphemus: [voice booming] Foreigners! Who are you? From where did you sail over these high seas? Are you thieves who have cast anchor on our shores?

[Man #1 and Man #2 shrink in terror]

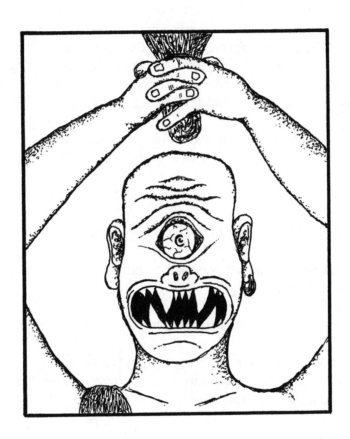

Odysseus: We are on our way back from Troy.

Polyphemus: What is your name?

Odysseus: My name is Nobody. We have been driven here by high winds and did not plan this visit. You know the mandates of hospitality; I ask you, dear sir, to remember them. Keep in mind Zeus is the travelers' god; he guards their steps and he guarantees them their rights.

Polyphemus: Stranger, you must be out of your mind to preach to me of fear for the gods. We Cyclopes care not for Zeus or any of the other gods. But tell me, where are your ships? I would like to see them.

Odysseus: [aside to the audience] He is trying to get around me, but I'll outwit him. [to Polyphemus] My ship was wrecked by Poseidon, the earthshaker, but my friends and I managed to escape.

Polyphemus: [jumping and screaming] I'll show you. [he bashes the head of Man #2 against the wall]

Odysseus: [taking out his bag of wine] Here, my friend, have some of this good wine.

Polyphemus: Wine? Let me have it. [drains the bag] There now! I'll take a sleep and deal with you fellows later. [slumps to the ground]

Odysseus: [to Man #1] Come, help me. Sharpen this tool. We will poke his eye out with this. [Man sharpens tool, while Odysseus checks door to cave and takes leather pouch away from the giant] Take the poker and together we will stab him in his one eye. [Odysseus and Man #1 hold the tool and jab it into Polyphemus]

Polyphemus: [in great rage] Help me! Dear father, Poseidon, save your son. These fools have blinded me. You will pay for this! [shrieking]

Cyclopes: [from offstage] What is the matter, Polyphemus? Who is hurting you?

Polyphemus: Nobody is hurting me. Did you hear me? Nobody is hurting me.

Cyclopes: If nobody is hurting you, we shall be on our way, but do not yell so loudly. It is disturbing the peace.

Polyphemus: [stumbles off stage left shrieking] Help me, help me! Nobody has blinded me!

Odysseus: [follows Polyphemus to exit and watches] He has positioned himself by the door of the cave so that he might grab us as we leave. Never fear. We will tie ourselves underneath the rams and leave with them.

[dim lights for a few seconds]

Odysseus: We made it. [to audience] We tied ourselves under two of the rams. The giant sat there and felt the tops of each ram. And he talked to them as if they were close friends. I could actually feel the breath of the Cyclops upon me. But let us hurry to the ship. [they walk briskly across stage but stop at left exit]

Polyphemus: [offstage] Come back, you fools. Come back. Come back, Nobody.

Odysseus: Cyclops! So I am not a weakling even though I may look it. [a great rock comes from off stage and barely misses Odysseus and men]

Man #1:	Aren't you imprudent to taunt this giant?
Odysseus:	[shouting] Cyclops, if anyone ever asks you who blinded you, tell them it was Odysseus, son of Laertes, who lives in Ithaca.
Polyphemus:	[from off stage] So the prophecy has come true. I was told that Odysseus would rob me of my sight but I thought it would be a large and handsome man and you are a puny little guy who confused me. But come here, Odysseus, so that I might ask Poseidon, who is my father, to help you on your way home. And he will heal my eye, too.
Odysseus:	I am certain even the earthshaker will not heal your eye.
Polyphemus:	Great father Poseidon, grant that Odysseus will never reach his home in Ithaca. But if he should get home, grant that he will find much trouble in his home. [again sends rock across the stage]

[curtain]

Act II. A year with Circe.

Beach on the island of Aeaea, home of the witch, Circe.

[curtain]

Enter Odysseus, from left.

Odysseus:	[looking over his shoulder at left entrance] Come men, shake off your doldrums. We may be miserable, but we are not down yet. [enter three men from left] East and west means nothing to us here. I climbed the peak yonder and saw that we were indeed on an island. We are surrounded by a vast sea. Where the sun comes from and where he sets we do not know.
Elpenor:	O, woe! I want to go home. I am so young.
Odysseus:	Do not lose heart, Elpenor. I saw a wisp of smoke coming from the center of the island which of course means that some humans are about.
All men:	[crying] We don't want anyone; we can't forget the past.
Odysseus:	But we must forget the past. It is true that we were almost home and I don't like to fix blame, but I did not open the bag of winds given to us by King Aeolus. It was some of you men who out of jealousy opened the bag thinking it was full of gold and precious gems. And the very wind that escaped from the bag brought us here.

Had you not opened the bag we would be home by now, as King Aeolus had gathered all the winds that would be harmful to us and put them in that bag. But come, let us rally our courage.

Man #1: Royal master, do you want to repeat the problems that we had when we landed near the home of the Laestrygonians?

Man #2: Yes, remember that dear Odysseus. From out of nowhere they appeared and threw great boulders at us, sinking ships and killing men.

Odysseus: We must take chances or we shall never see our homeland, our sweet homeland that is so dear to all of us. Come, be brave, put on the spirit of adventure. I now command you. [to Eurylochus] Eurylochus, you are of noble birth, so you will help me. We'll shake lots in this bronze helmet. The loser will take two men and investigate the island and the others will stay here with the winner. [they shake lots; Eurylochus loses and reluctantly exits left; dim lights for twenty seconds; when lights are brightened, Odysseus and Eurylochus are standing right front]

Eurylochus: My lord Odysseus, we followed your orders. We found a castle and could hear sweet singing coming from inside. My men gave great shouts and a beautiful woman came out. She invited us in. All the men went in, but suspecting a trap I stayed outside. The men never came back.

Odysseus: We must go and find out what happened to the men.

Eurylochus: My king, I do not wish to accompany you. You will be lost to us forever and you will not be able to rescue a single man. Leave me here.

Odysseus: Very well, Eurylochus, stay where you are, eat, drink and rest your bones, but I shall go. It is my plain duty.

[Eurylochus exits right]

Odysseus: [walks slowly from left to right, pausing now and then] I must find my men.

Hermes: [enter from left] Where are you off to now, my good fellow? Why are you wandering around this countryside alone when your friends are groveling in Circe's pigsty? I suppose you hope to free them but with your luck more likely you will end up in the pigsty yourself.

Odysseus: Who are you? Is this Circe you mention, the same Circe who turns men into animals?

Hermes: I am Hermes, sent here by Zeus. Yes, Circe is the witch who has it in her power to turn men into animals. The sad part is that they continue to think like men but have the bodies of animals. As I said, Circe has turned your men into pigs. However, I have been sent to the rescue and will see you through. [he hands a small amount of parsley to Odysseus] Here, take some of this herb, moly, and when Circe tries to turn you into a pig, she will not be able to do it. Eat it now.

Odysseus: I am speechless and thankful. [Hermes exits left and Odysseus, eating the parsley, continues his walk across the stage] I wonder what I am really up against here. Now that I've eaten the moly, of course I am not going to be intimidated by this Circe person. Hermes is right. It would be my luck to land on her island! She is notorious!

[Odysseus stands motionless while lights dim and brighten again]

Odysseus: Circe, Circe. Come outside. I would like to meet you.

Circe: [entering from right] Come in, sweet man. I would love to have you visit.

Odysseus: I will sit out here and talk with you.

Circe: Very well, give me a moment while I bring some refreshments. [exits left]

Odysseus: [to audience] We know what she is up to.

Circe: [enters from left, carrying golden cup and vial of magic potion] Please, drink some pottage from my golden cup. [she turns slightly so Odysseus cannot see her drop a magic potion into the cup]

Odysseus: Thank you, my fair lady. [he drains the cup]

Circe: [touching him with a wand] Off with you to the pigsty.

[Odysseus rushes at her with a sword and she falls to his feet]

Who on earth are you? What woman gave birth to such a man? I am amazed to see you take my potion and suffer no magic change. [pause] Please be gentle with me.

Odysseus: How can you expect me to be gentle with you? You, who have turned my friends into pigs.

Circe: I have no evil intentions toward you. Do you suspect a trap? Have no fear.

Odysseus: Could any honest man in my position bear to be happy while his men are imprisoned? Give my men their liberty and let me set my eyes upon them.

[Circe leaves stage and returns with the men; they weep for happiness, each one hugging the other]

Circe: I know as well as you, all you have gone through both on the seas and at the hands of monsters and evil persons on land. You are tired and sorely depressed. Stay here awhile and be refreshed. [Circe and men stand quietly in background]

Odysseus: [center front, talking to audience] I agreed to stay awhile and one day passed another. Soon a whole year had gone by, and my men became restless. One of my men even said "Master, if you are ever going to escape and get back to your old home in your own country, it's high time you thought of Ithaca again." This was enough for me and I approached Circe.

Odysseus: [backing up to center stage] Circe, I beseech you to help me go home. I am eager now to be gone and so are my men. They constantly beg me to take them home.

Circe: Kingly son of Laertes, Odysseus, the sharp-witted, I am not going to imprison you in my house against your wishes. But before I send you home you must make a journey to Hades to consult the soul of Teiresias, the blind prophet. You needn't be afraid of him. He still has his wits about him, although he is the only one in all of Hades that does.

Odysseus: This news breaks my heart. Tell me, Circe, who is to guide me. No one yet has sailed a ship into hell!

Circe: Don't worry about it. The North Wind will blow you across River Ocean and you should then beach your ship and walk into Hades. When you come to a spot where a branch of the River Styx pours thundering streams around a pinnacle of rock, you have found the right place. Dig a deep hole and pour in your libations to the gods. Now be off. [exits]

[men come from upstage and join Odysseus downstage]

Man #1:   [enters breathlessly from left] Sir, we have a problem. Elpenor just fell off the roof ...

Man #2:   Master, we must give Elpenor a proper burial.

Odysseus: Right now, we have no time. Circe said we must go. So come men. Circe said that we must first go to Hades.

Men: No, no. This isn't right. [much crying]

Odysseus: What is your problem?

Man #3:   It is Elpenor. How can we leave him? He not only lost his mortal life but unless we give him a proper burial his soul will wander. He will not be able to go to the Elysian Fields. [more crying]

Odysseus: I understand but we have no time right now. We will give him proper burial when we return as Circe says we must do after visiting Hades. Come, we must go quickly.

[curtain]

Act III. Hades.

Enter Odysseus, followed by three crewmen.

[curtain]

Odysseus: [to audience] We sailed past the River Ocean without incident, and finally came to rest at the foot of the pinnacles described by Circe. [backs up to center stage] Dig the hole here men. Make a deep trench. [men dig trench] From Hades will come the souls of the dead. Come, pour into the trench the blood of sacrificed sheep. [Odysseus' hands are stretched upward as he prays, while the men pour a liquid into trench] Gods, please hear your worthless servant. I promise when I return to Ithaca I'll sacrifice the best heifer in my palace and heap the pyre with presents. And to Teiresias I offer the finest sheep I own. [looking around] Stand back men. Here comes a ghost. [to the ghost, who earlier has leaned over and drunk from the trench] Elpenor, what are you doing here?

Elpenor: [big sigh] My royal master, the sharp-witted Odysseus, it was the master of some evil power that was my undoing. I fell off the roof, as you know, but because no one had time to weep for me or to bury me, I wander around. I beseech you, my prince, when you return to Aeaea, please give me a decent burial so that my soul can find rest. Raise a mound for me on the shore of the blue-gray sea, and on my barrow plant the oar I used to pull when I was alive.

Odysseus: [stretching his sword out above the blood in the trench] My dear Elpenor, I will do all of this. Nothing shall be forgotten. [Elpenor backs offstage left and a woman approaches the trench and sits down; Odysseus motions to her but she does not seem to see him; enter Teiresias, the blind prophet, who bends down and drinks from trench; he then approaches Odysseus, but does not cross the trench]

Teiresias: [holding a golden rod in his hand] Son of Laertes, Odysseus of the lively wits, what are you doing here? What possessed you to forsake the sunlight and come to this unhappy place? Take a step back from the trench so that I can drink the blood and prophesy the truth to you. [he leans over and drinks from the trench] My lord Odysseus, you wish your troubles were over and that quickly and without mishap you would be reunited with your family. But this is not to be. Your journey will be made hard. I doubt that the earthshaker will forgive you or in any way ease up on his relentless pursuit. But do not give up hope. You can reach home but not with comfort.

You must keep a tight rein on your men and specifically warn them about harming the cattle on Hyperion's island. If the cattle are in any way hurt, your ship will be destroyed, and if you do escape, you will arrive home in sorrow, upon a foreign ship and your men will be dead.

Odysseus: Teiresias, I cannot doubt that what you say is true. This is what the gods have declared for me. But there is another matter I do not understand. Over there sits my dead mother, or at least her soul is there. She sits in silence by the blood and says not a word to her son. What can I do to have her speak to me?

Teiresias: There is a simple answer, my friend. Any ghost you allow to drink the blood will talk to you. Without this, they will leave you and retire. [exits left]

Odysseus: [backing off from trench and replacing sword] Come, my mother, drink of the blood. [his mother drinks of the blood and immediately speaks to her son]

Mother: My child, how did you come to this drab and dingy place, you that are still alive?

Odysseus: I was forced by necessity to consult the blind prophet. But tell me. Why did the Fates send you here? How did death overcome you?

Mother: I died of a broken heart when you did not return from Troy.

Odysseus: [reaches out to touch his mother; twice she withdraws] Mother, why do you withdraw from me when I try to touch you?

Mother: My child, my child! You have so many sorrows. This is not a trick. You are only obeying the laws of our mortal nature. We no longer have sinews. Our bodies are not real. When you do arrive home, remember me to your dear wife and most beloved son. Goodbye my son.

Odysseus: [hands outstretched] Mother! Mother! [weeping]

[curtain]

Act IV. Scylla and Charybdis.

On board ship. Odysseus and three crewmen are on deck.

[curtain]

Odysseus: [downstage center, talking to audience] From the rushing waters of the River Ocean my ship passed into the open sea and without mishap reached the island where Circe lived. I immediately sent men to get Elpenor's body so that we could now give him the proper burial. While here, Circe gave me instructions as to how to deal with the dreaded singing Sirens, and Scylla and Charybdis. I listened carefully and it was a good thing that I did so. The Sirens would sing so beautifully that we would be tempted to join them. We should go to any lengths to avoid Scylla, the evil monster with dog heads attached to snake-like appendages and Charybdis, a whirlpool who sucked up ships!

[lovely singing in the background; the singing grows louder]

Odysseus: Quickly men, bind my hands to the mast. Hurry. I know I must be tied up or I will want to join them. Tie me tighter. [Odysseus throws himself against the mast and the men tie him] Put wax in your ears. Quickly get wax in your ears so that you do not hear them. [men hurry to get wax in their ears, the Sirens are louder] I cannot stand the strain. Beautiful voices! Let me loose. Men, let me loose. [he struggles to free himself of the bonds] I must hear those maidens. Take the ship ashore.

Man #1: [tying him tighter] We do only what you told us to do. I can't hear what you say Odysseus, but you struggle so fiercely, we should tighten you up.

Man #2: Forgive us, Odysseus, but you must not give in to this temptation.

[singing gradually fades and men untie Odysseus]

Odysseus: Thank you, men. You did just the right thing. [pause] But what is that cloud in the distance? [a terrible roar—the roar of an angry sea] Men, do not be frightened. We have met trouble before. Do exactly as I say. Strike those oars. Give it all the energy you have. With luck we can slip by without disaster.

Man #1: Master, where shall I steer the ship?

Odysseus: Give a wide berth to that smoke and surf you see. Take a middle course. Don't hug these cliffs, or before you can stop her the ship may take it into her head to make a dash over there and you'll wreck us.

Man #1: Odysseus. Help us! [terrified screaming] Save us! Scylla has snatched two men already! Help us! [loud groaning]

Odysseus: While I was busy watching Charybdis, Scylla got the best of us. Don't go near the edge of the ship. Stay in the center. Keep rowing, faster, faster.

Man #2: No, no. [great screams of terror, as he is grabbed by a huge arm]

Odysseus: Gods of Olympus, help us, help your mortal creatures. [pitiful sound] And we can't seem to get by Charybdis either. Men, row faster, we must get out of here. [pause; Odysseus looks carefully out at sea] Men, come here. Listen carefully to me for a moment. We are almost to the island of the sun god and Teiresias warned me repeatedly to keep clear of it. So row past it.

Eurylochus: Odysseus, you are one of those hard men whose spirit never gets low and whose body never gets tired. You must be made of iron to even suggest that we not stop for rest on this island. Let us rest here, cook our supper on the shore and sleep. We won't stray and in the morning we will get on board and put out to open sea.

Men: [applause] Yea! Yea!

Odysseus: I do not have the energy nor the inclination to fight you, but I ask every man to give me his solemn promise that if he comes across a herd of cattle that he will not touch any of them.

Men: Of course, we solemnly swear.

[thunder and lightning]

Odysseus: [walking to front of stage] Well, as you might have guessed, my men upset the sun god by eating the cattle. The storms kept raging and we were forced to stay over a month on the island, but as food ran out they became more restless and eventually gave in to temptation. Hyperion called upon all the gods to punish me. We put to sea. A terrible storm broke my ship in two. I managed to cling to a gigantic log and for nine days drifted until I landed on the island of Ogygia, the home of Calypso. All the other men aboard died.

[curtain]

Act V. The gods help Odysseus.

SCENE 1. Meeting of gods on Mount Olympus.

[curtain]

Athena: Father Zeus and you other merry gods who live forever, I have become convinced that it does not pay for kings to be kind, generous, and just. Look at Odysseus, that poor fellow! Today, not one of his subjects in Ithaca gave him a thought. No, he is left to languish on an island in misery. The enchantress, Calypso, has had him in her clutches for seven years and she sees that there is no escape. Not that he could reach Ithaca in any case, for he has neither ship nor crew to carry him so far across the sea. Has he found no favor in your sight? Why so much bitterness against him, father Zeus?

Zeus: Nonsense, Athena, my daughter. How could I put the good king Odysseus out of my mind? He is not only the most learned of men but he is also the most benevolent. It is Poseidon, the earthshaker, who is so against him on account of Polyphemus whom Odysseus blinded. Poseidon has been after Odysseus ever since but he stops short of killing him. At this council of gods let us put our heads together and figure out a way to get the poor fellow home. Poseidon cannot possibly hold out against the united will of the gods.

Athena: Father of ours, if it is really the pleasure of the blessed gods that the wise Odysseus shall return to Ithaca, let us send our messenger, Hermes, to the isle of Ogygia to tell Calypso that she must now set Odysseus free. My heart just aches for him.

Zeus: My child, I never thought I would hear such words from you. Why do you show such grief? But never mind. Hermes, come here.

Hermes: Yes, Father, gatherer of the clouds.

Zeus: Hermes, since you are the messenger, go at once to Calypso and tell her Odysseus must be set free. On the journey he shall have neither gods nor men to help him. His trip will be difficult and not without mishap, but he will eventually arrive on the island of the Phaeacians, those most respected kinsmen of ours, who will see that he is speedily escorted home in one of their special ships.

[curtain]

SCENE 2. Isle of Ogygia.

Odysseus sits on the ground, downstage left, in front of the curtain. Enter Hermes, followed by Calypso.

[curtain]

Calypso: Hermes, what brings you here? I am honored. Tell me what is on your mind and I shall gladly do what you ask of me, if I can and if it is not impossible. But first let me offer you some hospitality. [Odysseus stays seated and motionless]

Hermes: [accepts cup from Calypso] This is very good nectar. Really delicious! Very well, I will be frank. It was Zeus who sent me. He says you have the King of Ithaca here who has been dogged by misfortune. On the way home from the Trojan War, he was caught up in wind storms. He even lost all his loyal followers. And now Zeus bids that you let him off without delay.

Calypso: [trembling and obviously upset] How cold-blooded you gods are. Odysseus was driven to this island by wind and waves and I rescued him. Does this not count? If Zeus insists that Odysseus must leave, let him be gone across the dismal water. But he must not expect me to transport him. I have no ship, no oars, no crew to carry him so far across the sea. Yet I do promise to give him directions and send him on his way.

Hermes: Then send him off at once and so avoid provoking Zeus or he may be annoyed and punish you some day. And so, dear Calypso, I take my leave. [exit right]

Calypso: [to the audience] I must look for Odysseus. I believe I will find him at the seashore. He always sits for hours gazing out to sea, no doubt thinking of his home in Ithaca. There he is. [she moves toward him and puts her hand on his head] My unhappy friend, as far as I am concerned you may leave this island. I am ready with all my heart to help you do it. But you must be up and doing. Fell some tall trees and make a big boat. I shall fill it with provisions. I'll also give you clothing and send you a wind.

Odysseus: For years I made the mistake of trusting you. I have no confidence in you at all. Are you sure that you are not plotting against me?

Calypso: [she strokes his head again] Odysseus, what a villain you are to even suggest such a thing. It shows the sly manner in which your mind works. On the falling water of Styx, the greatest and most solemn oath the gods can take, I swear I hold no secret plan for your downfall. Come, let us go. [they move to center stage]

Odysseus: I must leave as soon as possible, for if I am away from home much longer, no one will recognize me, not even my poor wife or my son.

Calypso: I see you mean to leave more quickly than I desire. Even so I wish you happiness.

Odysseus: I long to see my home and celebrate the happy day of my return. What if the powers that be wreck me at sea? I will endure that too, for in my day I have had many bitter experiences at sea. So let any new disaster come.

[dim lights for twenty seconds]

Odysseus: [to audience] It was a joyous day when I left. I followed the stars as Calypso had told me to do, but Poseidon spotted me when he was on his way back from Ethiopia. He was furious and decided to really finish me. He gathered the clouds together and grabbed his trident, stirring up the sea in his great wrath. Eventually, I lost my boat and had only a raft. Poseidon sent a mighty wave and I was tossed off the raft.

Knowing that my only hope was swimming to shore, I started in slow, deliberate strokes. I finally made it, with just the energy to cast myself upon the sand and sleep.

[curtain]

Act VI. Odysseus meets Nausicaa.

SCENE 1. Beach on Scherie.

[curtain]

Odysseus is sleeping off to the left, in front of the curtain. Princess Nausicaa, daughter of King Alcinous of Phaeacia, is playing ball with her three maids. The girls are laughing and making playful squeals. Odysseus sits up and rubs his eyes.

Odysseus: [to the audience] Alas, where have I been cast ashore? Who are these folks? Some savage tribe or kindly people? And what is this shrill cry in my ears, as though some maidens were at play? Can these human beings talk as I do? I must find out. [Odysseus creeps closer; he sees the girls and bursts upon them, sending all, except Nausicaa, running to hide in terror]

Nausicaa: Sir, you have frightened my maids. Just who are you to be so bold?

Odysseus: Mistress, I beg your mercy. Are you a goddess or are you one of us mortals who lives on earth? If so, lucky indeed are your father and your gentle mother. But about me? Only yesterday, after the nineteen days at sea that it took me to come from Ogygia, I was tossed and almost drowned upon these shores. Take pity upon me. I beg you to direct me to the nearest town and please give me some linens to wrap around myself. And in return may the gods grant you any desire.

Nausicaa: Sir, your manners being excellent, proves to me that you are no rascal. I will tell you who we are and I will show you to the city. The country and the city you will see belong to the Phaeacians. I myself am the daughter of King Alcinous, who is the head of our state. [turns toward her maids] Stop, my maids. Why are you cringing at the sight of this man? Don't tell me you take him for an enemy, for there is not a man on earth who would dare to set hostile feet on Phaeacian soil. Don't you know that we are under the protection of the gods and that all travelers are protected by gods? Hurry up, give this guest food and drink, and while he bathes, please fetch him some clothes. [maids exit right]

Odysseus: Please excuse me while I wash off the brine. [he steps offstage to the left]

Nausicaa: Listen, my dear maids, while I tell you what I have been thinking. This man is here because of Olympian powers. When I first met him, I knew there was something special. I do believe he is here at the direction of Zeus. Last night I dreamed about this. In my dream I was told to gather up all my clothes and the clothes of my brothers and come here today to wash them. My father the king provided a cart to bring us here and my mother filled the cart with food.

Odysseus: [enters wearing a splendid cloak] Thank you, my dear maiden for this magnificant cloak.

Nausicaa: Say not a word, sir, but come. It is time to start our journey to the city. I will direct you to my good father's palace where you will meet the nobility. But this is how we might do it. I believe you are a man of understanding and will realize why I must give you these instructions. While we are in the country, walk along with my maids, but once we are near the city I want you to drop back and not be seen with us. It would not be good for anyone to see me with you. They would say "Oh, there is Nausicaa. Who is that man with her? Is it her husband-to-be?" I do not want to cause talk. So you stay in a pleasant grove of trees that I will point out to you. When you think we have had time to arrive home, you walk into town and ask the way to King Alcinous's palace.

[curtain]

SCENE 2: Palace of King Alcinous.

King Alcinous and his wife are seated on thrones. Three others from the court stand nearby.

[curtain]

Odysseus: [enters and walks to front of stage] It was hard for me to do but I walked straight into the palace and knelt before the king and queen. Athena had made me bold. [turning toward Queen Arete and King Alcinous] I seek refuge with your lord.

King: Stand up my good fellow. You have obviously come from afar. [to a servant] Have a feast prepared. Let us get comfortable.

Odysseus: I beg you to arrange to have me taken to my own country. I long to see my wife and son. I have had to live through many a long day of hardship since last I saw them.

Queen: Listen to this poor creature.

King: [to a waiter] Mix a bowl of wine and fill the cups of all the company in the hall, so that we may now make an offering to Zeus, who watches over all those who deserve respect, and I am sure that this man does. Now, I ask you all, should we give this man safe passage home? [cheers and ayes from the group] But tell us sir, who are you?

Odysseus: [walks toward front of stage] I am Odysseus, son of Laertes of Ithaca. It is a harsh land but I for one know of no other sight, other than one's own country, that brings such tears of joy to one's eyes. I have a long tale to tell ...

TEACHERS' NOTES

1. Use transparency number 1 on overhead projector. Ask the students what part of the world they see. As they give you the answers write on transparency: Southern Europe, Near East, North Africa, and the Mediterranean Sea. Point out the Black Sea, which, in the earliest days, the Greeks called the Euxine Sea. Ask if anyone can show you where the following islands are located: Sicily, Malta, Ithaca, Crete, and Cyprus. Give the students a blank map and have them color all water a light blue. Now they are ready to locate the above places on their own maps.

2. Tell the students that this was the world as the Greeks saw it. The River Ocean flowed around the world in both directions. Put transparency number 2 on the overhead projector. Point out that these are the locations important in the play they are about to read. Hades was someplace outside the River Ocean in the stories of Homer. That means if Odysseus had to cross the River Ocean, he had to leave the Mediterranean Sea. At what place did he sail out of the Mediterranean?

3. Hyperion (the sun god) lived near the banks of the River Ocean in the east and rode its current home each night in a golden cup. Some stories say that Hyperion lived in the Far West near the River Ocean.

4. Odysseus is the hero of this story. Some accounts say that as a young king, Odysseus was madly in love with Helen and was determined that he would marry her. In order to make himself look good to her father he saw to it that all Helen's suitors swore to avenge her if one day any outrage was committed against her or her future spouse. Helen caused the problem by choosing to marry Menelaus instead of Odysseus. Later this very scheme resulted in Odysseus having to lead his men into the Trojan War.

5. Mark the cities of Troy and Sparta on the map. Tell the students that Odysseus, king of Ithaca, led his men to Troy at the request of Agamemnon, brother of Menelaus of Sparta. Agamemnon rallied all those he could to help avenge his brother, because Paris had stolen Menelaus' Helen and taken her to Troy.

6. Ethiopia is often mentioned in mythology and does not refer to the country as we know it today. It is believed by some mythologists that Ethiopia refers to an area near Joppa, a place still within the world as the Greeks knew it. Still others say that Ethiopia was just south of Egypt.

7. When animals were sacrificed to the gods, the gods did not eat the meat, but they did like the aroma from the smoke. The people making the sacrifice ate the meat.

Transparency Master no. 1

RIVER OCEAN

THE
UNDERWORLD

(SICILY)
SIRENS
THRINACIS
• SCYLLA
• CHARYBDIS
OGYGIA
(MALTA)

MT.
OLYMPUS

THRACE

• TROY

ITHACA

SPARTA •

CRETE

CYPRUS

RIVER OCEAN

Odyssey Transparency Master no. 2

VOCABULARY

appendages. something that is attached or grows out as a natural but less important part of a whole

barrow. a heap of earth or rocks used in olden times to mark a grave

benevolent. kind, generous

cascade. a small, steep waterfall

dogged. refusing to give up, steady and determined

doldrums. a condition of feeling sad, bored

heifer. a young cow who has not given birth to a calf

hostile. having or showing hatred or dislike; unfriendly

immortal. never dying; living forever

intimidate. to make afraid; to force to do something or keep from doing something by frightening

languish. to become weak, lose energy, droop

luxuriant. growing thick and healthy; lush

mandate. an order or command

pinnacle. highest point, as of a mountain

prophecy. something told about the future, as by a prophet

pyre. a pile of wood on which a dead body is burned

sinew. tendon

solemn. serious, grave, very earnest

stature. the height of a person

vast. very great or very large

ACTIVITIES

1. Have the students draw on a large piece of construction paper (copy transparency master no. 1) the map of how the Greeks viewed the world. Locate the places where Odysseus visited. Tradition tells us that the Ciconians lived on the southwestern coast of Thrace. The singing Sirens, and the monsters Scylla and Charybdis were located between Sicily and the boot of Italy. The Cyclopes lived on Sicily and Calypso on the Isle of Malta. Hyperion, the sun god, kept his cattle on Thrinacis, thought by some mythologists to be the east coast of Sicily and by others to be a separate island. For the other places the students may use their imagination. Scherie could have been just about anywhere since distance meant nothing to the Phaeacians because they had special speed boats which they used to take foreigners home. Of course, the speed boats were god-powered, not mechanically powered. The Ciconians, the Lotus-eaters, and Laestrygonians are listed as people visited by Odysseus, but they are only barely mentioned in Homer's book and few details are given. When you have all the places on the map connect them using a marking pen.

The route of Odysseus:

1. leaves Troy	8. Underworld
2. Ciconians	9. singing Sirens
3. Lotus-eaters	10. Scylla and Charybdis
4. Cyclopes	11. sun god
5. king of the Winds	12. Calypso
6. Laestrygonians	13. Phaeacians
7. Circe	14. Ithaca

2. Write a descriptive essay of Odysseus's homeward journey putting all events in chronological order.

3. Have two teams of three each go to the blackboard. Have the letters in the names of characters, monsters, and places scrambled on a transparency. Using an overhead projector, uncover one name at a time. The first student to write the name correctly scores a team point. An incorrect spelling lowers the team score by one point. When score reaches ten, the high scorers are declared the winners and two new teams take their places.

4. Tape a radio show, complete with announcer and commercials. See production notes for puppet show in the general activities chapter. Do everything but the puppets.

5. Read "The Quest for Ulysses" (*National Geographic*, [August 1986]:197). This article recounts the experiences of Tim Severin who retraced the route of Odysseus in modern times. Give an oral report to the class. Use visual aids.

DISCUSSION QUESTIONS

Name _____

The Odyssey **Act I**

1. When Odysseus sent a few men to explore the land of the Lotus-eaters, what did the men do?

2. Who is the father of Polyphemus?

3. How did Odysseus blind Polyphemus?

4. What god is considered the traveler's god?

5. What in the story gives the clue that Odysseus has been a long time at sea?

6. How did Odysseus display his cunning nature?

7. Odysseus mentioned the laws of hospitality. What do you think they are?

8. Research the Erinyes (Furies).

Name _____

The Odyssey **Act II**

1. Why is Elpenor afraid to go ashore to explore the island Aeaea?

2. What did Odysseus see that made him realize that there is life on the island?

3. Why did some of the crew open the bag of winds given to Odysseus by King Aeolus?

4. What did the Laestrygonians do to Odysseus and his ships?

5. What in the story tells you that the voyage to Hades will be an arduous one?

6. Why did giving Elpenor a proper burial seem so important?

7. How did Circe break the laws of hospitality?

8. Research the Graces.

Name _____

The Odyssey Act **III**

1. What did the men pour into the trench they dug?

2. What does Odysseus promise the gods he will do when he arrives in Ithaca?

3. What does Elpenor tell Odysseus he wants on his grave?

4. What warning did Teiresias give Odysseus about the island of the sun god?

5. How do you know that Odysseus's mother was upset when he did not return on time from the Trojan War?

6. How do you know Odysseus feels sad when he talks to his mother?

7. Why is Odysseus referred to as "Odysseus of the lively wits?"

8. Pretend you are Odysseus. After leaving the Underworld, write a letter to your son and describe the ordeal.

Name _____

The Odyssey Act IV

1. Why did Odysseus have himself tied to the mast?

2. Why did Odysseus have the crew put wax in their ears?

3. Who are Scylla and Charybdis?

4. How do you know that Odysseus was a strong man?

5. What mistake in judgment did Odysseus make that ultimately cost the lives of all the crew?

6. What evidence is there in acts I-IV that Eurylochus is a coward?

7. What does it mean to say someone is caught between their own personal Scylla and Charybdis?

8. You are a crewman aboard Odysseus's ship. Write a page in the log telling of the day's events.

Name _____

The Odyssey Act V

1. Who does Zeus say is really against Odysseus?

2. Who is Zeus's messenger?

3. What ultimatum did Hermes deliver to Calypso? Have you ever been given an ultimatum?

4. What does Zeus say the Phaeacians will do for Odysseus?

5. How did Calypso break the rules of hospitality?

6. Why is Calypso unhappy at Hermes directive?

7. Why is Odysseus suspicious of Calypso's motives?

8. Research the Olympian gods. Make a chart showing their Greek names, Roman names, and what their positions are. Why do Hestia and Hades not have a throne?

Name _____

The Odyssey **Act VI**

1. Who is Nausicaa?

2. What are the girls doing on the beach when Odysseus hears them?

3. How would you have handled the sudden appearance of Odysseus if you were Nausicaa?

4. Why does Nausicaa not wish to be seen with Odysseus?

5. Why would there be no one on earth who would set hostile feet on Phaeacian soil?

6. What do you know about Nausicaa's character?

7. How does the king show a respect for the laws of hospitality?

8. Use your imagination. Have Odysseus's ship stop at an imaginary island of your own making. Whom does he meet? How is he treated? What does he do?

TESTS

Name _____

The Odyssey Test Yourself

Using the words below, fill in the blanks. Each word will be used once.

Nausicaa	Ithaca	Teiresias	Nobody
Elpenor	Polyphemus	Calypso	Circe
River Ocean	libation	Hermes	River Styx
Eurylochus	Scylla	singing Sirens	Charybdis
Odysseus	Zeus	Poseidon	Aeolus

1._____Cloudgatherer.

2._____Son of Laertes.

3._____Cyclops.

4._____Odysseus called himself this.

5._____She kept Odysseus seven years.

6._____Crewman of noble birth.

7._____Messenger of gods.

8._____A witch.

9._____He fell off roof.

10._____The Earthshaker

11._____It flows in two directions.

12._____Blind prophet.

13._____Liquid offering to the gods.

14._____They lured sailors by their songs.

15._____Monster with six heads.

16._____Whirlpool.

17._____Princess who befriended Odysseus.

18._____Homeland of Odysseus.

19._____Keeper of the winds.

20._____Mortals swear by it.

Name_____

The *Odyssey* Final Test

( )   1.   The homeland of Odysseus was: (a) Scherie (b) Ogygia (c) Ithaca.

( )   2.   The river that flowed in two directions was: (a) River Ocean (b) River Styx (c) River Lethe.

( )   3.   The earthshaker was: (a) Poseidon (b) Zeus (c) Hermes.

( )   4.   In order to recognize her son the mother of Odysseus had to: (a) cross the trench (b) drink blood (c) be given a tap with the golden rod.

( )   5.   This monster sucked up ships: (a) Sirens (b) Scylla (c) Charybdis.

( )   6.   Elpenor needed to be properly buried or his soul would: (a) wander aimlessly (b) be sent to the Elysian Fields (c) returned to Circe.

( )   7.   The messenger of the gods was: (a) Athena (b) Arete (c) Hermes.

( )   8.   Aeolus was the: (a) keeper of the winds (b) sun god (c) twelve-footed monster.

( )   9.   A true witch was: (a) Circe (b) Calypso (c) Nausicaa.

( ) 10.   One who had nimble wits was: (a) Elpenor (b) Alcinous (c) Odysseus.

( ) 11.   Odysseus was returning home from the: (a) Trojan War (b) Greek War (c) War of the Roses.

( ) 12.   The voyage home lasted for: (a) three years (b) ten years (c) nine years.

( ) 13.   Giants with one eye were called: (a) Ciconians (b) Cyclopes (c) Phaeacians.

( ) 14.   Nausicaa told Odysseus to: (a) ride all the way to the palace with her (b) not to come at all (c) wait in the forest and walk to her father's palace later.

( ) 15.   When the men ate the lotus leaves they: (a) started fighting (b) became forgetful (c) slept.

( ) 16.   The famous river in Hades was: (a) River Ocean (b) River Styx (c) Eel River.

( ) 17.   Elpenor died: (a) by choking to death (b) because he was so lonesome (c) by falling off the roof.

( ) 18.   Circe turned the men into: (a) pigs (b) turtles (c) cattle.

( ) 19.   The sun god did not want anyone to disturb his: (a) rabbits (b) cattle (c) horses.

( ) 20.   Odysseus was: (a) very short (b) very tall (c) average.

MYTHO GAME

See instructions in the chapter on general activities, page 228.

1.   What does one call a large fire for burning a corpse?

2.   Name the island which is the homeland of Phaeacians.

3.   What is a word for craggy mountains with high points?

4.   On what island did Circe live?

5.   Who was king of the Phaeacians?

6.   Who is the keeper of the winds?

7.   Who is the sun god?

8.   Name an herb which made one immune to the spell of witches.

9.   Name the mountain where the gods lived.

10.   What did the gods drink?

11.   Name the island on which Calypso lived.

12.   Who is the brother of Menelaus?

13.   Name the goddess of wisdom.

14.   How many years was Odysseus held captive by Calypso?

15.   Name the king of Ithaca.

16.   Name the daughter of Alcinous.

17.   What is the liquid offering to the gods?

18.   Name gigantic men and women who threw boulders at Odysseus's ships.

19.   What is Odysseus's home?

20.   Who is the messenger of the gods?

21.   Name a nobleman who was on Odysseus's crew.

22.   Poseidon was on his way home from this place when he spotted Odysseus on his homemade craft.

23.   What crewman fell off Circe's roof?

24. Who was the one-eyed giant that Odysseus blinded?

25. Name the whirlpool that sucks up ships.

26. Name the witch who turned men into pigs.

27. Where does King Aeolus live?

28. Who are the people who live in Scherie?

29. Who is the god of the sea?

30. Who is King Alcinous's wife?

31. Name the creature who has twelve feet, six necks, and six heads.

32. Who is the blind prophet?

33. Who is the cloudgatherer?

34. Who is the earthshaker?

35. Name the place where Hyperion kept his cattle pastured.

36. For how many years did Odysseus try to get home?

37. When the men ate the lotus blossoms, what happened to them?

38. Who are the very first people that Odysseus met on his journey?

39. Give the name used for an extended journey or wandering.

40. How many years did Odysseus stay with Calypso?

41. What did Odysseus offer the Cyclops?

42. What did Odysseus hide under when escaping from the Cyclops?

43. When the ships arrived at Circe's island, what did Odysseus see that was reassuring?

44. What must the ghosts in the Underworld do before they can speak?

45. What did the crew put in their ears to keep them from hearing the singing Sirens?

46. Who owned the cattle that the blind prophet warned Odysseus not to bother?

47. Odysseus was returning from what war?

48. Who brought the message to Calypso that she was to release Odysseus?

49. What is the name of the whirlpool that lives off Sicily?

50. What did Poseidon grab when he was stirring up a storm?

THE ODYSSEY CROSSWORD PUZZLE CLUES

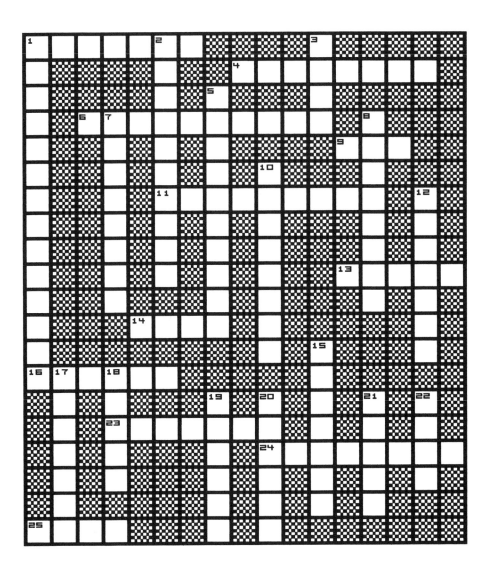

Across

1. Father of Odysseus
4. God of the sea
6. Odysseus poked out his eye
9. Kept crewmen from hearing the Sirens
11. Whirlpool
13. God of the underworld
14. Circe turned men into _____
16. Six-headed monster
23. Poseidon's symbol
24. Sun god
25. A special herb

Down

1. They threw boulders at the ships
2. Nobleman, member of the crew
3. King of the gods
5. Gentle people, kinsmen of the gods
7. King of Ithaca
8. Daughter of King Alcinous
10. Crew ate his sacred cattle
12. He fell off roof
15. The gods lived here
17. She kept Odysseus for seven years
18. Eating the blossoms caused forgetfulness
19. Messenger of the gods
20. Odysseus was a native son of this land
21. A witch
22. City at war with the Greeks

THE PLAY

Cast of Characters
In Order of Appearance

Narrator
Jason, leader of the Argonauts
Chiron, a wise Centaur
King Pelias, usurper of Aeson's throne
Adviser, court of Pelias
Hercules, strong man
Orpheus, musician
Zetes, son of Boreas, the North Wind
Calais, brother of Zetes
Hypsipyle, leader of women in Lemnos
Theseus, famous Athenian king
Phineus, old prophet
Castor, son of Leda, protector of sailors
Pollux, brother of Castor
Hera, queen of gods
Aphrodite, goddess of beauty
Eros, son of Aphrodite
Voice of Ganymedes, Olympian cupbearer
King Aeetes, king of Colchis
Boy, king's grandson
Medea, daughter of King Aeetes
Talus, bronze man who lives on Crete
Alcestis, daughter of Pelias
Pelopea, daughter of Pelias

Prologue

[curtain]

Narrator stands in front of curtain at left side. Jason and Chiron stand quietly on stage while narrator speaks.

Narrator: Chiron was a good Centaur, or I should say the good Centaur, as the rest of the Centaurs were a wild group without manners. Living in a cave at the foot of Mount Pelion, Chiron was entrusted by many families to bring up their sons. Jason was one of these. This scene opens the day Jason is about to leave his kindly tutor.

Jason: Goodbye, Chiron. You are a wise and kind Centaur. I will never forget your kindness to me. When I have recovered my rightful place as a king in Greece I will reward you.

Chiron: Never mind the rewards. It was my happiness to be a part of such growth. You have understood my words and followed my directions. It was indeed my pleasure to have had you in my company all these years.

Jason: I will remember what you have told me about being reasonable and keeping my cool.

Chiron: Yes, that is important. In all your dealings, think first and then act. We have all heard of Hercules and his great strength and courage. But he does not think first and in the end this could be his undoing. So my dear charge, remember to use your head.

Jason: After having you as my teacher for so many years, I think that is pretty much cemented in my mind. Think first.

Chiron: And be kind, be kind. Sometimes it is hard to be this. You are strong, athletic, handsome, and courageous. These things without kindness are nothing. So give this some thought.

Jason: I must be on my way. Goodbye, dear Chiron, until we meet again.

Chiron: Off with you, Jason. Safe trip. [Jason exits left and Chiron bows his head]

[curtain]

Act I. The beginnings.

Narrator: Jason walks swiftly down the mountainside. Coming to a river he finds an old lady sitting on the bank. He questions her and finds that she cannot get across the stream because it is too deep and swift for her. He takes her in his arms and carries her across the stream. She becomes heavier as he goes and at one point he stumbles and loses one sandal. The old lady thanks him for his generosity and as he puts her down she touches his arm. He feels the velvet touch and raises his eyes to look at her. She is gone; he has carried Hera and this he will not regret.

SCENE 1. Palace of King Pelias.

King and two advisers are talking; a servant is standing at front left.

Pelias: I was told by my oracle that I would die at the hands of a kinsman and that I should beware any man wearing a single sandal.

Adviser: The man that has just come to town is wearing only one sandal but he certainly doesn't look like a threat.

Pelias: [agitated voice] Why do you say that? What does he look like?

Adviser: He wears a well-fitting garment and he has a leopard's skin thrown over his shoulders.

Pelias: And his body?

Adviser: His bright hair is hanging down his back. He is muscular and quite handsome. He carries himself well.

Pelias: I must see for myself. [beckons to servant] Bring this fellow of which we speak to see me. Tell him the king demands his presence. [exit servant] You all know of course that my uncle had a son, whom he sent off somewhere. I never could find out where. It seems my uncle, the former king, wished for his son to rule. This, of course, was wishful thinking on his part. I am upset because of what my oracle said to me. But here they come now. [he goes over to right exit as Jason and servant enter]

Jason: Welcome me to your palace, dear cousin.

Pelias: Why do you call me cousin? What country is your native land? Don't lie to me. Don't stretch the truth. Be totally honest. I beg you. Tell me the truth.

Jason: [gently] This is my father's homeland. I made this journey to recover the land that is rightfully his. I am indeed your cousin. My name is Jason, although that is a name more recently given to me. My birth name is Diomedes.

Pelias: So you are Diomedes, son of Aeson and Polymele. I thought you were long dead.

Jason: No, I am quite alive as you can see. You and I must be governed by truth. We must not use swords and spears to settle our differences.

Pelias: What do you mean?

Jason: That we should not fight. We should do what is right. Keep all the gold you acquired. Keep the sheep and cattle. Keep the pastures and the green fields, but give to me the throne which is rightfully mine.

Pelias: So be it. But before I do this, something must be done.

Jason: And what is that?

Pelias: Phrixus died in Colchis. There, too, is the Golden Fleece. You are a strong lad, so before settling down to affairs of state, enjoy a good adventure and an adventure that will bring its own reward. Bring back the Golden Fleece. This will put the spirit of Phrixus to rest.

Jason: [incredulously] You want me to bring back the Golden Fleece?

Pelias: The oracle thus spoke. You are still a youth. With Zeus as a witness, I will give you the kingdom when you return to me the Golden Fleece. You will spend your time here with me of course while you are preparing for your voyage.

Jason: If you will be so kind, could I go to my room and refresh myself?

Pelias: [beckening to servant] Come take Jason to his room and see to it that a great feast is prepared. We have an honored guest. [Jason and servant depart, the king walks to downstage center and addresses the audience] I have no intention of honoring this promise. I do not need to worry because Jason will never return from this quest. It will be dangerous indeed and, in fact, impossible. But the youth will not realize this and so in the end I will be the victor. [pauses] I can afford to be polite to my cousin.

[curtain]

SCENE 2. Room in the palace.

Present are Hercules, Zetes, and Calais.

Jason: I do not go into this thinking that I will be doomed, rather I go with feelings of adventure and courage. However, there is always the possibility of disaster. Hercules, what do you say?

Hercules:	You know, Jason, of my many exploits. I am strong and love a challenge, and it is with great anticipation that I accompany you. When I heard of this voyage I immediately stopped what I was doing and hastened to be with you. My armor-bearer, Hylas, will also make the trip. [enter Orpheus, unseen by the others] But I can't figure out why you are willing to have Orpheus go with us.
Jason:	It is because of his marvelous music. When he plays the lyre and sings, all else is unimportant. His music may even be our savior. Men and beasts are tamed by his tone. You'll see. I won't compare you, only to say that you are physically strong but he has the soft touch.
Orpheus:	[stepping forward] Thank you, Jason, for your defense. It is from my mother, Calliope, one of the Muses, that I get that soft touch, the love of music and poetry, and the ability to put the words in symphony.
Jason:	Well said, Orpheus. We are glad to have you with us.
Hercules:	I will be anxious to hear this music and my apologies to you sir.
Zetes and Calais:	[in unison] And why have you included us in your crew?
Jason:	You are likable, honest men and, well, let's face it, you are the sons of Boreas, the North Wind. What better help can we get than a strong wind upon occasion?
Hercules:	[interrupting] Surely, we will not fit in one of the standard small boats. What are your plans in this regard?
Jason:	We are having a big ship built, big enough for fifty men.
Zetes:	[anxiously] But won't it be too heavy? Won't it sink?
Jason:	Not the way it is shaped. It will be one of the wonders of the world. We will call the ship *Argo* after the builder and we will be the Argonauts. I've invited the builder, Argus, to accompany us. Since the builder will be aboard, he will do his very best to make it seaworthy.
Narrator:	And so Jason's ship was finished some eleven months after its beginning. The young men of Greece joyfully met its challenge. Among the crew were Castor and his brother, Pollux; Achilles's father, Peleus, and of course Hercules, Hylas, Orpheus, Theseus, Zetes, and Calais. They sailed away one sunny day with all the townspeople out to bid them goodbye.

[curtain]

Act II. The voyage.

SCENE 1. Lemnos, an island inhabited only by women.

[curtain]

Enter Jason, with Hercules and Orpheus.

Jason: There seem to only women here. This is peculiar.

Hercules: Yes, I see them from a distance. They look quite strong. I wonder what happened to all the men.

Jason: Here comes one of them. [enter Hypsipyle, the leader] Please, forgive our intrusion. We are looking for a place to spend the night. We wonder if we will be welcome as we notice there are no men here.

Hypsipyle: All but our old king, who is my father, are dead. We are strong women. We liberated ourselves from the likes of men. This does not mean that you cannot stay here or that you are in any danger from us. We will leave well enough alone and allow you to set up camp here for the night, or for as many days as you wish to stay.

Jason: I am impressed with your attitude. Could we meet your father?

Hypsipyle: This is impossible as we set him afloat in a small craft. Hopefully he found his way to safety.

Hercules: You really are serious, although you do not seem to have much heart.

Hypsipyle: That is a rash judgment on your part. We could not keep my father. He understood that. We are fiercely determined not to be dominated by men, but on the other hand we can be good hostesses. We will prepare your food and wine and have some fresh garments ready for you in the morning.

Jason: The men will respect you and indeed we give you our thanks.

[curtain]

SCENE 2. An island with only one inhabitant, a lonely old man.

Narrator: It wasn't long after leaving Lemnos, that Hercules caused a problem. The Argonauts cast anchor at a nearby island and Hylas, the armor-bearer, leaned over a pond in order to dip a pitcher into the spring. A water nymph threw her arms around his neck and pulled him under. Hercules was disconsolate and sought him madly everywhere. When he did not find him, Hercules did not return to the ship. The Argonauts finally had to leave without him but only after much sorrowful debate. Later in the day, they came upon another desolate island.

[curtain]

Jason: Come men, we will beach here for the night. Tie up the *Argo*. Drop anchor.

Theseus: I see an old man, barely able to crawl. He is over yonder. [Theseus points to left; Jason, Zetes, and Calais turn to look in that direction] See he can barely move.

Jason: [Jason approaches left, leans down and supports old man] What is the matter, old fellow? You look very hungry. What is your name?

Phineus: My name is Phineus. Some time ago, I displeased Zeus and now I am being punished.

Jason: It is always better not to incur the displeasure of the gods. What did you do?

Phineus: Apollo gave me the gift of prophecy. Admittedly I did not use this gift wisely. I made the mistake of telling Hera what Zeus planned to do on earth. Zeus really became upset. He said it was bad enough to have Hera on his tail without me giving her the proper clues. It was frightful. I beg of you to help me.

Jason: What can we do for you?

Phineus: From my gift of prophecy I know that two men, the sons of Boreas, can defend me against the Harpies. You see, as soon as I prepare myself some food these birds swoop down and take the food and then while they are flying away they give off a foul and sickening odor. No human can stand it. That is why I live here all alone.

Zetes: Since you have the gift of prophecy, you know that my brother and I are aboard the *Argo*. We will gladly help you.

Calais: We will stand on either side of you and when you are given your dinner and the Harpies swoop down we will chase them and kill them, for being the sons of the North Wind we are faster than lightning.

[dim lights for a few seconds]

Zetes: We chased the dreadful monsters. We caught up with them and clubbed them for a fare thee well.

Calais: Just as we were about to finish them off, Iris happened to be coming down her rainbow and she stopped us. She begged us not to harm these birds as they were special to Zeus. But she swore by the water of the River Styx, an oath that can never be broken, that they would never again harm Phineus.

Phineus: My happiness knows no bounds. Three cheers. Let us feast and celebrate. I will repay you by telling you about your future trip. Gather closer. [men move closer to Phineus] You must watch out for the Symplegades, the clashing rocks who continually roll against one another. You must carefully make your way through. First have a trial run with a dove. If she passes through safely, more than likely you will pass through safely also. If the dove does not get through … But then let us not think negatively.

[curtain]

SCENE 3. Aboard the *Argo*.

Jason: Man the oars. Everybody to his station. I see the Symplegades ahead. Ready the dove for release. Orpheus, start playing your lyre. [Orpheus begins playing]

Theseus: The men are ready, Jason. I don't see how anyone can get through those rocks. Look how they batter each other.

Jason: As they separate, we will release the dove. [Jason leans further out to have a good look] Let the dove fly. Let the dove fly.

Pollux: It is done as you said. The dove is flying through the rocks.

[Orpheus plays and men scan the horizon to watch the dove]

Jason: The dove is through safely, losing only one tail feather. Get ready the next time they part. Go, men, go. Row harder, Orpheus, play louder. Your sweet music will inspire the men. Go men.

Castor: I think we are going to make it. Faster! Faster!

Jason: We are safe. Men, we made it through the Symplegades.

Theseus: Look back. The rocks are not moving. The clashing rocks are as if they are asleep.

Jason: Behold, the rocks are stuck together. They came at us so hard that they stuck together. May they stay that way forever and never again assault the men that sail the sea.

[curtain]

Act III. Mount Olympus.

Narrator: Not long after this episode the sailors passed the land of the Amazons, warrior women they would have loved to engage in battle, but the winds were just right so they reluctantly passed up the temptation. Nothing further interrupted their voyage and a few days later they reached Colchis, the country of the Golden Fleece. In the meantime, on Mount Olympus some of the goddesses were showing concern for the voyagers.

[curtain]

Hera: [to audience] I am sick with concern for Jason. I have promised myself that I would see him through this ordeal. It is so difficult. Zeus is away and it keeps me busy just watching out for him, too, and seeing to it that he does not make a fool of himself. Yes, the most powerful god must be watched. Even though Aphrodite and I don't get along very well, I must ask her for assistance. I think she can help me. [calls to maid] Please ask Aphrodite to come by and see me when she has time. After all I am wife of Zeus....

Aphrodite: [entering from left] Hera, did you wish to see me. I got your message just as I was leaving my palace so I thought I would come by now.

Hera: Dear Aphrodite, do come in and make yourself comfortable.

Aphrodite: [to audience] She calls me dear? She must want something.

Hera: I am really concerned about Jason and the Argonauts. There are at least fifty fine Greeks aboard the *Argo*, the cream of Greek society, one might say. I am worried.

Aphrodite: What can I do? You and Athena have been keeping your eye on them. I am more beautiful than resourceful, as all the gods on Olympus know. So why do you call upon me to help?

Hera: They have just arrived in Colchis, the country of the Golden Fleece. I thought perhaps you and I could come up with an idea.

Aphrodite: I feel quite honored that you would ask me. How do you think I could help?

Hera: The king of Colchis has a daughter, Medea, who is a natural born magician. In fact, she is a priestess of Hecate and besides that her aunt is Circe, the witch. So you know what that means. She is good! If she were to fall in love with Jason, then she would certainly use her knowledge of magic to help him gain the Golden Fleece.

Aphrodite: I get it. You want me to instruct my son, Eros, to shoot the magic arrow containing the love potion at Medea.

Hera: That's it. Have Eros shoot the arrow so that the first person that Medea looks upon after the shooting will be Jason. Then she will not be able to help herself. She will be madly in love and will do anything to help Jason.

Aphrodite: This is truly a fine idea. Now I have only to deal with Eros. He can be such a recalcitrant son. Let me think a moment. [pauses and puts her hand to her temple] Ah, I have it. I will promise to give him a lovely plaything, a beautiful ball of blue and gold. I will call him now, as I left him outside your palace. [calls out door, upstage left] Eros, Eros, come in here. I want you.

[enter Eros carrying two oversized dice]

Voice: [offstage] You cheat! You're a dirty cheater. I don't want to play with you anymore anyway.

Aphrodite: Who is that, Eros?

Eros: That is Ganymede, you know, the royal cupbearer. He always says I cheat, but you know I would not do that, Mother.

Aphrodite:	Of course, you would not cheat. Now listen to me.
Eros:	Yes, Mother. I am all ears.
Aphrodite:	Say hello to Queen Hera, son.
Eros:	Hello, Queen Hera. Do you have any ambrosia? Do have anything for me to play with?
Aphrodite:	Mind your manners, son. We called to you because we have a job for you.
Eros:	[hangs his head] No, I am tired of your jobs. I like to play and you are always having me doing love jobs for you. What did you do before I was born?
Hera:	[to Aphrodite] He is quite bold for one so young. Aphrodite, I do believe that you let this little fellow have too many liberties. He is too sure of himself.
Aphrodite:	Shape up, Eros, or Mother will not get you a new plaything. If you do as I say I will see that you have a lovely gold ball that will be just yours. All the gods will ask "Where did Eros get that ball?"
Eros:	[brightening] Yes, what do you want me to do?
Aphrodite:	Fly to Colchis and find the maiden, Medea. Just before she looks upon Jason of the Argonauts, shoot an arrow into her heart, so that she will fall madly in love with him.
Eros:	That is easy. I am off. [starts out door left]
Aphrodite:	Report back to me as soon as you arrive home. Queen Hera and I will be waiting for you.

[curtain]

Act IV. Jason and the king of Colchis.

SCENE 1. The palace.

Narrator:	The heroes found their way to the palace of the king of Colchis. Hera had clothed them in a rainy mist so they were unseen until their arrival at the palace gates. King Aeetes was not thrilled with the visit but he hid his feelings and welcomed them, not asking them who they were and why they came until after they had bathed and had dinner.

[curtain]

King:	So now that you are refreshed, please tell me who you are and from where do you come?
Jason:	We are all men of high birth. Our heritage is one of kings. We came from Greece. We come seeking the Golden Fleece. If you will help us in this endeavor, we will provide you with any service you request.
King:	Indeed. Your request is not simple, although that it might seem.
Theseus:	We know it is not simple. That is why we offer to do anything. We will even fight your battles for you, if that is what you wish.
King:	[to audience] I am annoyed. I do not like outsiders. I want to be left alone in peace. If these fellows had not just feasted with me, I would kill them all. [to Jason and the crew] I bear you no ill will. You are all bold men. I have heard of many of you as tales of your exploits come even to these far eastern shores of the Euxine sea.
Jason:	We will do whatever you say.
King:	I will give you a task. If you prove your courage I will give you the Golden Fleece.
Jason:	Well said. What shall we do?
King:	I have two bulls whose feet are of bronze and who breathe fire. You are to put a yoke around their necks and plow the field. Then the teeth of a dragon must be sowed, like seed corn, from which will spring up an army. You must fight these soldiers as they come toward you and put them all down. [Jason and his men look at each other in consternation] Come now! This isn't too much. I've done this myself.
Jason:	[sits speechless for a moment, then rises] I will do it. Come men we must go back to the ship. [all follow after Jason as he exits left]
King:	So we shall see who is brave.

[curtain]

SCENE 2. Aboard the *Argo*.

Present are Jason, Theseus, Castor, Pollux, and Zetes.

Narrator:	As you might have guessed, Medea, out of curiosity, had sneaked into the courtyard to view the handsome strangers. Eros was there and just at the opportune moment he shot an arrow into her heart. She is now fortunately in love with Jason, who is unaware of this new love interest.

[curtain]

Theseus: Jason, this expedition should not chance losing its leader. Please let me handle this.

Jason: Wait a minute! Wait a minute! What kind of a coward do you think I am? I could never transfer this burden to you. I, too, am strong.

Theseus: I used the wrong words. Believe me, I never would deliberately offend you. I want only that you continue to lead the Argonauts and this challenge given by the king is very risky business, as he intends it to be. I certainly know that you are not a coward.

Zetes: Either my brother or myself should go. We are fed by the North Wind and will never fail. Our father would see to it.

Jason: Enough! I will do it. You are brave men and I appreciate your concern but I will do it. [a knock on the door] See who is at the door. [Zetes opens door and welcomes a young boy] Come in, boy. Don't be afraid. What can we do for you?

Boy: I am taking a chance coming here so I must be quick. I hear a great deal of discussion at the palace and I can help you.

Jason: And how do you propose to do this?

Boy: Listen to me. My aunt, Medea the king's daughter, has magic powers that enable her to do anything. Just ask the moon and the stars! She can do anything.

Theseus: But how do you know that Medea will help us? We are nothing to her.

Boy: We don't know for sure but perhaps she can be persuaded. If so, you will be able to conquer the bulls and do anything.

Zetes: Jason, it is a chance that we should take. Why don't you go ashore and visit Medea. You have nothing to lose.

Jason: Only my head, if a guard finds me lurking around the palace and doesn't recognize me.

Boy: I will walk with you to her door and that way no guard will bother you as they will know me.

Jason: It is worth a try. I will go with you.

[curtain]

SCENE 3. Medea's Room.

Narrator: Of course Jason and his comrades do not know that Medea has already been smitten with Jason and will do anything that he desires. We find Medea alone in her room.

[curtain]

Medea: My heart is torn between love for Jason and the loyalty to my father, the king. I know what the king is asking will lead to Jason's death if I do not intervene but can a daughter betray a good father in such a manner? If the gods would only tell me what to do. [she breaks down in sobs, but quickly dries her tears upon hearing a knock at the door; she opens the door and Jason and the boy enter]

Boy: Aunt Medea, I have brought Jason to meet you. You know that my grandfather, the king, has given him an impossible task. I told Jason about your magic powers and we now come to you for help. [Medea cannot take her eyes off Jason]

Jason: It is with great pleasure that I meet you, fair Medea. You are indeed more beautiful than I have been led to believe. It is with a most earnest desire that I beg you to help me.

Medea: I want to help you, Jason. You are noted for your courage and strength but I doubt that you could complete my father's task without a catastrophe. I am torn between you and my father, who deserves my loyalty.

Jason: To help me would be hard. To deny would be death. Please see in your heart the means to assist me.

Medea: Your words twist me into shreds. [pause] I will help you. I will give you a box of ointment [she takes it from where it is tucked inside her dress at the throat] When this is rubbed on your weapons it will make you and your weapons invincible for the day. If too many of the dragon-teeth men come at you, throw a stone in their midst and they will instead turn upon each other. Go now. You must not be seen here.

Jason: I will never forget you. Come to Greece and you shall be worshiped for this.

Medea: I will remember you forever. [Jason and the boy exit left] May the gods forgive me for this treason against my father, the king. [she bows her head]

[curtain]

Act V. Aboard ship.

SCENE 1: Jason, Theseus, Orpheus, and Zetes are aboard ship.

[curtain]

Narrator: Jason, because of the magic ointment was able to subdue the bulls, sow the dragon's teeth, and reap the harvest. As directed he threw a stone into the midst of the armed men who sprang up from the sowed teeth. The contest ended in victory for Jason. King Aeetes was furious, and he secretly vowed revenge. In the meantime, Medea, overcome with love and misery, sneaked out of the palace and sought Jason on his ship.

Jason: Well, we did it. We conquered the bulls. The Golden Fleece is ours.

Zetes: I don't like to spoil the good time, but we do not have it in our hands.

Jason: Ah, but there is no reason to suspect that King Aeetes is anything but honorable. He has treated us with the utmost courtesy.

Zetes: That in itself makes me suspicious. We came to take the prized Golden Fleece from him and yet he treated us like visiting royalty.

Theseus: You call the treacherous game he put Jason through treating him like royalty? I have another word for it.

Jason: Let us not argue among ourselves. It is a time of celebration. Who do I hear climbing up the ladder? [he goes to exit left as Medea enters practically falling into his arms]

Medea: Please take me with you. I have to go with you to Greece.

Jason: [lifting her from her knees] What is this all about? Why are you in such anguish?

Medea: My father is very angry. He vows that you will never have the Golden Fleece. There is no reason to say that it was promised you, for he has no intention of keeping any promises to you.

Jason: You are his daughter. If anyone knows this man, you do. What shall we do?

Medea: Go after the Golden Fleece tonight. It is guarded by a vicious serpent but with my magic powers I will calm it and lull it into sleep.

Jason: Now is the time for rejoicing. Certainly you will go to Greece with us and once there I will make you my wedded wife. But now let us listen to your plan.

Medea: [to Jason] We will go together, just the two of us. The others will stay here and get the ship ready to sail. Have all the men ready to row as soon as we put our feet aboard. In the meantime, you and I will approach the dragon. I will sing a special lullaby to it and within minutes you will hear the monster snoring. As soon as this happens, you will take the Golden Fleece off the tree on which it is hanging and we will return to the ship before the monster awakens.

Jason: You are a valiant and spirited woman besides being most beautiful. Come, let us go.

[curtain]

SCENE 2. At sea aboard the *Argo*.

On stage are Jason, Medea, Theseus, Zetes, and Calais.

Narrator: Jason and Medea did get the Golden Fleece as planned but they did not plan on meeting her brother, Apsyrtus. The king, having been alerted to the problem, sent Apsyrtus to stop Jason and Medea from escaping. Medea killed her brother. The stories told are several, some saying that Medea did the actual slaying and others saying that she set him up for Jason. But whatever, she was responsible for his death, a horrible deed. The gods do not look kindly on one who kills his own kin, so in order to be freed of such guilt Medea persuaded Jason to take her to visit her aunt, Circe, who would be able to cleanse her. This added additional weeks to the voyage and took the Argonauts close to the forbidding monsters, Scylla and Charybdis.

[curtain]

Jason: We will soon be passing between Scylla and Charybdis. Medea, stay away from the railings. Sit here in the middle. I do not want to subject you to any danger. [to Zetes] Tell Orpheus to get his lyre ready. [Zetes exits right]

Medea: My place is with you. I love you, Jason, and I want to be with you no matter what danger we are in.

Jason: No arguments now. I love you and I want you to stay seated right where you are.

Orpheus: [enters right] Do you want me to play?

Jason: Yes, immediately, and as loud as you can. [Orpheus strums lyre]

Theseus: On the left I see the six-headed monster, Scylla. Keep the ship out of her reach. [loud screams] Hera, please watch over us and guide us.

Jason: Not so far to the right. The whirlpool! Charybdis is snarling and spitting. See how she sucks up water. Pray to the gods that she does not suck us up.

Theseus: [leaning over the rail] I see a very promising sight. Some beautiful sea nymphs. They can only be out here to help us. Hera has heard our prayers. Do you feel the ship change its course?

Jason: Yes, the sea nymphs have lifted us clear out of the water. [men huddle together to keep their balance]

Medea: What is happening to us?

Jason: The goddess, Hera, sent us help. The sea nymphs are guiding us through this terrible strait. Let us rejoice. We are saved.

Medea: Don't be so sure. We are not in Greece yet.

Jason: Medea, have faith. We will get home.

[dim lights for a few seconds]

Jason: There is the island of Crete up ahead. Make way to pull close to shore and drop the anchor.

Medea: Jason, I implore you, do not go ashore on Crete.

Jason: Why, dear heart?

Medea: There is a man named Talus who lives on this island. He is the last man left over from the bronze race. Take a look quickly. There he is on the shore.

Jason: You are right. He is terrible to behold.

Talus: [yelling from offstage] Get away from my island or I will crush you with rocks. Do not get any closer. [a rock is hurled across the stage]

Medea: Dreaded hounds of Hades, hear me! Come and destroy this Talus who seeks to wreck our ship. Hounds of Hades, hear me! I'll stare at him and hypnotize him.

Jason: Look, this old bronze Talus, as you called him, just hurt himself while he was trying to throw a boulder at us. He cut his ankle and look at the blood gush out. He really fixed himself.

Theseus: Yes, with a wound bleeding like that, it won't be long before he dies. Mean as he was, I dislike to be a witness to death.

Jason: I don't feel that way. Without his death we would be dead. And I will vote for his any day.

Medea: He is gone. The hounds of Hades helped us.

Jason: Let us go ashore where we can rest and ready ourselves for our journey home.

[curtain]

Act VI. Jason and Medea in Greece.

SCENE 1. A palace sitting room.

Narrator: The *Argo* arrived in home port. Each hero went his separate way to his home and Jason and Medea hurried to the palace of Pelias with the Golden Fleece. They found that Pelias had forced Jason's father to kill himself and that his mother had died of grief. Jason, bent on avenging this wickedness, turns to Medea for help.

[curtain]

Enter Medea followed by the king's daughters, Alcestis and Pelopea.

Medea: So you two young ladies would like to get to know me better. The feeling is mutual, I, too, wish to know you.

Alcestis: Yes, we do. We do know that you are the daughter of King Aeetes of Colchis, but that is all we know. What do you like? What are your hobbies?

Medea: Well, I do like children and I hope some day to have a family.

Pelopea: But what do you like to do with yourself?

Medea: I like magic.

Pelopea: Do you mean that you can perform magic tricks?

Medea: Well, I do know how to make someone old become young again.

Alcestis: Show us, please show us.

Medea: Well, it can't be done immediately. I must go to visit Hecate and get just the right materials. Give me some time. I'll take my winged chariot and take the journey to the dark side of the moon.

Alcestis: It is so exciting. Just think, a trip to the dark side of the moon. How long will you be gone?

Medea: I'd say nine days, give or take a few hours.

[dim lights for twenty seconds]

Medea: Well girls, I have had a most successful trip. Hecate was miserable as usual, but she gave me what I needed. Let me see. Into the pot goes the blood of a calf. Now we dance around the pot three times. That's it. Here, take a branch [hands branch to each girl] and help me stir. Good! Now gravel and leaves from far away places, snow scooped up from wayside drifts, a bat's left wing, and the entrails of a shark. Give it a little stir, girls! Next we put in two peacock feathers, one vulture's claw, and finally the ground livers of three lambs. A little of this and a little of that! We can't rush this as it must simmer for about twenty-four hours. Come back tomorrow.

[dim lights for a few seconds]

Medea: So here we are again. This will take just a while longer. After a bit I'll put in a ram that is so old it is almost dead. You will see a lovely young lamb get out of the pot. The potion will rejuvenate the ram.

Pelopea: This is wonderful. If it works ...

Medea: [interrupting] If it works? Of course it works.

Pelopea: I'm sorry. I was going to say that if it works could you do it for my father, King Pelias? He is old and soon we will lose him. We would like him back as a youth.

Medea: Of course, it will be no problem. I'll fix him up a sleeping draught and you can put it in his wine. Then he will sleep and you can ready him for the pot. When he gets out of the pot he will be a handsome youth, as he was in his early days.

Girls: This is a happy day.

Narrator: It turned out to be not such a happy day. Medea convinced the girls and they in turn gave their father a sleeping potion. Then they cut him up and put him in the pot even though the whole affair was extremely distasteful. And of course, this time, Medea had not put in the magic herbs or cast a spell over the contents, so not-so-good King Pelias went to his eternal reward sooner than expected. Immediately thereafter, Jason and Medea moved to Corinth where we encounter them now in their sitting room.

[curtain]

SCENE 2. A room in the palace.

Enter Jason, followed by Medea.

Medea: You brought me here from Colchis to make me your bride. Now you tell me that you want to marry the daughter of the king of Corinth! What kind of man are you? After all I have done for you, you treat me this way. Now you forsake me? Where shall I go? Back to my father's house? To Pelias's daughters? I have become for you the enemy of all.

Jason: I owe you nothing. It was Aphrodite who saved me. She had her son Eros shoot his arrow into your heart just as you first laid eyes on me. From then on you were out of control. I do not owe you. You owe me for bringing you to Greece, a country that is civilized.

Medea: Get out of my sight. If you think for one minute I'll let you go without a fight, you are crazy. I'll get that beautiful princess and she will regret that she was ever born. She is nothing but a hussy.

Jason: Do not threaten like that or the king will have you banished. I know him and he will not tolerate any bad talk about his daughter.

Medea: Get out. Now.

Jason: Medea, take some gold and settle in a new place before you bring down the wrath of both the king of Corinth and the gods.

Medea: Get out!!! [screams]

Jason: You have too much pride for your own good. I'm gone. [Jason exits left]

Medea: [Medea walks downstage center and faces audience] So this is the way it is to end? Well, I'll see to it that there is more to the ending than he bargains for. I will send his bride a beautiful gown. It will be exquisite and she will not be able to resist it. [She walks over and takes a beautiful gown out of chest] I'll anoint it with special potions. She will be sorry.

Narrator: Yes, everyone was sorry including Medea. You might say that she was run out of town. In her winged chariot she flew to Athens where she became the wife of King Aegeus. But let me not say more, because you will meet her again in our next tale about Theseus, and I wouldn't want you to be prejudiced.

[curtain]

TEACHERS' NOTES

1. Use transparency number 1 on the overhead projector. Review the parts of the world according to the Greeks: Southern Europe, Near East, North Africa, and the Mediterranean Sea. Ask if any one of the students can place the following: Thessaly, Lemnos Island, Hellespont, Iolcus, Colchis, Corinth, and Sicily. Using transparency number 3, familiarize the students with the above places and Jason's route. Give the students a blank map and have them color the water a light blue and then locate the places on the map and mark the route. Have them mark the spot where Jason encounters the Symplegades and the monsters, Scylla and Charybdis.

2. Give the students background of the story. Phrixus, a young Greek and some say his sister, Helle, were put on the back of a golden ram which supposedly was to carry them to safety to some far distant land where they would be out of the clutches of a wicked stepmother. Helle slipped and fell into the water when they were crossing the strait that separates Europe and Asia. This strait was then called Hellespont. Phrixus, however, made it to Colchis, where he sacrificed the ram to Zeus and gave the Golden Fleece to King Aeetes. Later, Phrixus's uncle, King Aeson, had his kingdom taken over by a nephew, a man named Pelias. Jason, son of Aeson, was sent away for safety to be brought up by the kindly Centaur, Chiron. We meet Jason as he leaves the care of Chiron and undertakes to establish himself as a rightful heir.

3. The Centaurs are half man and half horse and are reportedly rude, loud, and boisterous. Chiron was the only Centaur with a quiet, gentle manner.

4. Jason's voyage was probably the first big expedition. Ordinarily the boats were small, made from hollowed trees. Here, however, we have a ship large enough for fifty men. There were few facilities on board other than room for the men to sit at their oars and row. Each night the ship would try to put in at a cove or some such sheltered spot. After setting sail from Iolcus, Jason kept close to the shore until he had to sail out to the open sea, his first stop being the island of Lemnos.

5. On Jason's return trip he passed the singing Sirens, and the dreaded monsters, Scylla and Charybdis. Colchis is generally said to be at the far end of the Black Sea which puts Circe way off a normal route, but some versons of this story have Jason going out of his way to visit Circe on the way home. He could have easily been blown off course and put in the vicinity of the monsters. And since these tales were handed down, we can feel sure they got changed in the retelling.

6. Point out to the students that this expedition offered a challenge to men. Heralds proclaimed the news of the voyage and men came from some distance and backgrounds to participate. The accounts differ as to who actually was aboard, but it is generally agreed that all in this play were aboard with the exception of Theseus who was in some accounts but not all.

7. Some versions of the tale have Jason completely under the spell of Hypsipyle, leader of the women of Lemnos, even to the point where he wishes to forsake his quest of the Golden Fleece and remain on the island. This version has Hercules ordering him back on the ship.

8. Some accounts have Phineus a king in a splendid palace but unable to eat because of the miserable Harpies. Some tales have him as an old man alone.

9. Ask the students if they can tell you what the Hellespont is called today (the Dardanelles).

Golden Fleece Transparency Master no. 3

VOCABULARY

agitate. to disturb or excite the feelings of

anguish. great suffering as from worry, grief, or pain

assault. sudden attack with great force

banish. to force a person to leave his country as a punishment

destiny. that which is bound to happen

draught. a drink

episode. incident that forms part of a whole story

exploits. daring acts

inspire. to cause or influence to do something by example or word

intervene. to come in so as to help or settle

intrusion. the act of forcing oneself or one's thoughts without being asked or wanted

invincible. cannot be beaten

liberate. to free oneself or someone else

mutual. done or shared in common

quest. a journey in search of adventure

recalcitrant. stubborn, disobedient

rejuvenate. to make young or fresh again

tolerate. to put up with, endure, allow to be

valiant. brave, courageous

wrath. great anger, fury

ACTIVITIES

1. Make a map of Jason's voyages. Put map on a large piece of construction paper. Mark the place from which he left, and the places he visited both coming and going. Make a small illustration to indicate what took place at each stop. These small illustrations can be either done directly on the map or on pieces of art paper of various colors. The art paper can be cut into two-inch pieces and after the illustration is finished the pieces can be pasted on the map in the proper place. Connect the places using a marking pen.

2. Have the students write a paragraph in which they contrast Jason and Odysseus. Their topic sentences might be "Although Jason and Odysseus both made long voyages, they were dissimilar in many ways."

3. Write an essay chronicling the events of Jason's life.

4. Make a poster, pretending you are Jason and advertising for volunteers. Make sure the poster is eye-catching, tells where the sign-up is to be, when the voyage starts, where it is going, what it hopes to accomplish, and who is to be the leader.

5. Design a scene from the play.

   a. Select the scene

   b. List the characters in the scene and write a short character sketch, first describing the physical aspects of the character and then describe his or her personality.

   c. Design the costumes on art paper.

   d. Write a brief description of plot development in the scene.

   e. Design a mythological cover and staple the report.

6. Give an oral report on "Jason's Voyage" (*National Geographic*, [September 1985]: 406). Tim Severin and volunteer crews rowed the whole route of Jason. Make visual aids to go with report. Have the student make a quiz for classmates on subject matter.

7. Write an essay about the article in *National Geographic* comparing and contrasting the voyage of Jason and voyage of Severin.

DISCUSSION QUESTIONS

Name_____

The Golden Fleece **Prologue and Act I**

1. What is a Centaur?

2. Who told King Pelias that he would die at the hands of a relative?

3. Why is it important that Jason lost a sandal?

4. Why is Orpheus invited to be one of the Argonauts?

5. Do you think Jason is using Orpheus?

6. All of the Argonauts think adventure is an important aspect in life. What do you think?

7. How does King Pelias show a lack of integrity?

8. Using examples, write a paragraph in which you detail the marks of a good teacher or the kind of teacher that you would like to have in your class.

Name_____

The Golden Fleece Act II

1. What is strange about Lemnos?

2. Who is the leader on Lemnos?

3. Describe the Harpies.

4. What did Harpies do to Phineus?

5. When the ship neared the Symplegades, what clues told you the men were well drilled for the event?

6. Have you ever been in a "near impossible" situation in your life? Tell about it.

7. How do you know that Phineus knows ahead of time that the sons of the North Wind are aboard the *Argo*?

8. Research Hercules and his twelve labors in order. Read about one labor and draw a comic strip illustrating that one labor.

Name_____

The Golden Fleece Act III

1. What keeps Hera so busy?

2. How many Greeks are aboard the *Argo*?

3. What special qualities does Medea possess that will make her useful to Jason?

4. Why is Hera being so friendly to Aphrodite?

5. How do you know that Aphrodite is aware that Hera is using her?

6. Do you think Eros is spoiled? Do you know any spoiled children?

7. Does Eros seem honorable? Why or why not?

8. Eros and Cupid refer to the same god. Research and find out what you can about the background of this god.

Name_____

The Golden Fleece **Act IV**

1. How did Hera make it possible for the Argonauts to arrive at the palace unseen?

2. What did King Aeetes say that Jason must prove before he would give him the Golden Fleece?

3. How might Medea's life have been different had she not been shot with the arrow?

4. What events in the story could be fact?

5. How did Aeetes show he respected Greek customs?

6. Does Aeetes's grandson show more loyalty to his grandfather or Jason?

7. Why does Jason seem to feel insulted when Theseus wants to do the impossible task?

8. Write a paragraph comparing Jason and Odysseus.

Name_____

The Golden Fleece Act V

1. Why is Zetes suspicious of King Aeetes?

2. What message does Medea bring to Jason?

3. What does Jason promise Medea?

4. How does Medea propose to handle the dragon?

5. What does Medea do to Talus to quiet him?

6. How do you know that Hera is fond of Jason?

7. What indicates that Jason might be naive?

8. Research Asclepius (called Aesculapius by the Romans). What is the significance of the Caduceus?

Name_____

The Golden Fleece Act **VI**

1. What does Medea tell the daughters of King Pelias about herself?

2. Where does Medea go to find the herbs and other ingredients that she needs?

3. What do the girls want Medea to do for their father?

4. To whom does Jason say he owes all his good fortune?

5. What in this scene indicates that Jason may be mean-spirited?

6. How were the two daughters of King Pelias tricked?

7. What shows that the two daughters trusted Medea?

8. Research Symplegades, Scylla, Charybdis, Harpies, and Argus.

TESTS

Name_____

The Golden Fleece Test Yourself

From the list below select a word that best fits in the blank.

Calais	Scylla	Iris	Styx
Amazons	Medea	nymphs	Charybdis
Phrixus	Chiron	Ambrosia	Hylas
Hera	Harpies	Colchis	Orpheus
Hypsipyle	Eros	Zeus	Olympus

1._____Jason reclaimed the Golden Fleece thereby freeing this man's spirit.

2._____He reared Jason.

3._____Country at eastern end of Euxine Sea.

4._____Even animals stopped to listen to his lyre.

5._____One of the sons of the North Wind; his brother was Zetes.

6._____She led the independent women of Lemnos.

7._____Evil, foul-smelling, bird-like women.

8._____Strong warrior women.

9._____A six-headed monster who threatened ships.

10._____The rainbow was her skyway.

11._____A whirlpool who sucked up ships.

12._____Food of the gods.

13._____He was a good shot with the arrow.

14._____She had magical powers.

15._____The gods lived here.

16._____They carried Jason's ship to safety.

17._____A river in Hades.

18._____Chief god.

19._____Hercules abandoned ship because of him.

20._____Queen of gods.

Name_____

The Golden Fleece Final Test

Choose the correct answer and put the corresponding letter in the parentheses.

( )   1.   Aboard the *Argo* were : (a) thirty men (b) twenty men (c) fifty men.

( )   2.   The Argonauts sailed for: (a) Sicily (b) Ithaca (c) Colchis.

( )   3.   The main witch in the story was: (a) Circe (b) Hecate (c) Medea.

( )   4.   Eros rolled dice with: (a) Zeus (b) Ganymedes (c) Jason.

( )   5.   Orpheus' music inspired: (a) Sirens (b) Amazons (c) the crew.

( )   6.   The Centaur who cared for Jason was: (a) Chiron (b) Apsyrtus (c) Eon.

( )   7.   Armor-bearer to Hercules was: (a) Aeetes (b) Peleus (c) Hylas.

( )   8.   The given name of Jason was: (a) Diomedes (b) Ganymedes (c) Eros.

( )   9.   The whirlpool who sucked up ships was: (a) Scylla (b) Symplegades (c) Charybdis.

( )   10.   For their food the gods loved: (a) nectar (b) ambrosia (c) libation.

( )   11.   The chief god was: (a) Zeus (b) Athena (c) Iris.

( )   12.   Jason was happy to have Zetes and Calais aboard the *Argo* because their father was: (a) the West Wind (b) the North Wind (c) the Hurricanes.

( )   13.   Jason had to plow a field and sow: (a) dragon's teeth (b) horse's hooves (c) pieces of lamb fleece.

( )   14.   Talus, the last of ancient bronze men, was hurt: (a) on left side of head (b) by pulling his hair (c) on his ankle.

( )   15.   Hypsipyle set her father to sea in: (a) a boat (b) a casket (c) an old tree hollow.

( )   16.   Aphrodite asked Eros to shoot an arrow through the heart of: (a) Iris (b) Medea (c) Polymele.

( )   17.   Jason and Medea: (a) lived happily ever after (b) broke up soon after arriving home (c) broke up after fifteen years of marriage.

( )   18.   Medea: (a) had a winged chariot (b) rode on back of a serpent (c) asked the sun to take her in his chariot.

( )   19.   A place where the Greeks went to consult the deities was: (a) an oracle (b) a temple (c) a garden.

( )   20.   The goddess who felt responsible for Jason on his voyage was: (a) Aphrodite (b) Athena (c) Hera.

MYTHO GAME

See instructions in the chapter on general activities, page 228.

1. Give the name for the creature that was half man and half horse.

2. Who is noted for his strength but not necessarily his brains?

3. Who was the leader of the Argonauts?

4. Who was Jason's uncle?

5. Where did Greeks go to seek the gods' help?

6. What is Jason's given name?

7. Who is the father of Jason?

8. Who is the mother of Jason?

9. Who rode the ram to Colchis?

10. What is the present name of the Hellespont?

11. Jason went to Colchis to reclaim what?

12. Who is the chief god?

13. What celebrated musician was aboard *Argo*?

14. Name the sons of the North Wind.

15. Who was Hercules' armor-bearer?

16. Who was king of the Colchians?

17. Name the island where only women lived?

18. Name the leader of the determined women who lived alone.

19. Name a river in Hades (one often takes an oath on this river).

20. Name the evil bird-like women who stole food of Phineus.

21. Who is the last of the Bronze men?

22. Who is a prophet who told Jason what to expect?

23. Who is the goddess who slid down rainbows?

24. Who were the warrior women whom Jason didn't stop to fight?

25. What is the name given to the clashing rocks?

26. Name the country on eastern shore of the Euxine Sea where Jason was headed.

27. On what mountain did the gods live?

28. How was Jason's boat propelled?

29. What character in the play was the witch who helped Jason?

30. Name Aphrodite's son who was handy with arrows.

31. What cupbearer on Olympus rolled dice with Aphrodite's son?

32. Name Medea's brother.

33. Name a six-headed monster who lived on a rock.

34. Name the whirlpool who sucked up ships.

35. Who carried Jason's ship past the whirlpool?

36. Give a word that means stubborn, balky, difficult.

37. Give another word for search, expedition.

38. Give a word that means intervene, interfere, butt in.

39. Give a word, a noun, that means a prediction, a forecast.

40. Give a word that means control, domineer, overbear.

41. Give a word that means signal, summon, call.

42. Give a word that means stimulate, animate.

43. Give a word that means to open up, broaden, shower down upon.

44. Give a word that means occurrence, incident, happening.

45. Give a word that means pose, posture, position.

46. Give a word that means deed, act, achievement.

47. Give a word that means attack, assail.

48. Give a word that means defenseless, susceptible.

49. Give a word that means powerful, unyielding.

50. Give a word that means anger, fury.

THE GOLDEN FLEECE CROSSWORD PUZZLE CLUES

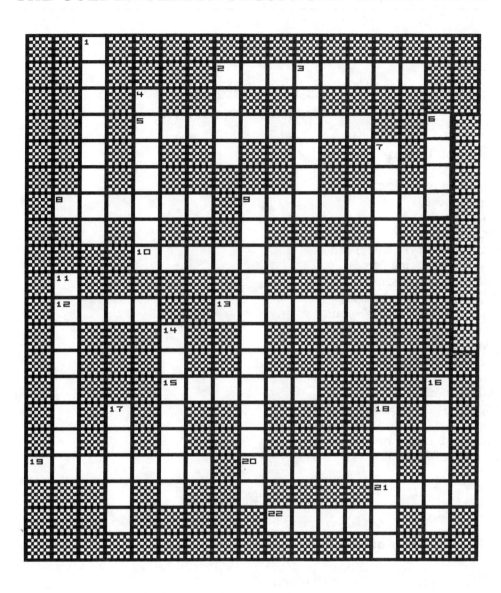

Across

2. Strong man
5. Goddess of beauty
8. Usurper of King Aeson's throne
9. Olympian cupbearer
10. Clashing rocks
12. Jason's ship
13. Only women lived on this island
15. Brother of Castor
19. Half man and half horse
20. Son of Leda
21. Son of Aphrodite
22. Daughter of King Aeetes

Down

1. Given name of Jason
2. Queen of gods
3. Wise Centaur
4. Foul-smelling bird-like women
6. Instrument played by Orpheus
7. King of Colchis
9. Object of Argonauts' voyage
11. One of the Muses
14. Musician, son of Calliope
16. Chiron lived at the foot of this mountain
17. Son of the North Wind
18. The North Wind

The Greatest Athenian

THE PLAY

Cast of Characters
In Order of Appearance

Aethra, mother of Theseus
Theseus, son of Aegeus of Athens
Grandfather, king of Troezen
Medea, wife of Aegeus
Medus, son of Medea
Aegeus, king of Athens
Daedalus, architect of the Labyrinth
Ariadne, daughter of King Minos
Crewman #1, aboard Theseus's ship
Crewman #2, aboard Theseus's ship
Man #1, nobleman of Theseus's court
Man #2, nobleman of Theseus's court
Adrastus, king of Argos
Pirithous, king of Magnesia
Antiope, queen of the Amazons
Adviser, Athenian court
Hippolytos, son of Antiope and Theseus
Phaedra, another daughter of Minos
Hades, king of the Underworld
Hercules, cousin of Theseus

Act I. The Youth.

SCENE 1. Room in palace of King Pittheus of Troezen.

Aethra and Theseus are talking to each other.

[curtain]

Aethra: [patting the sofa] My son, come here and sit next to me. It is time that I told you the truth about yourself.

Theseus: What do you mean, dear mother? Haven't you always told me the truth?

Aethra: I have never directly lied to you, but when you asked me about your father, I talked in circles and never gave you the complete truth.

Theseus: [sitting down next to his mother] Tell me, Mother.

Aethra: Theseus, your father is Aegeus, the king of Athens. [Theseus moves closer to his mother] Since today is your sixteenth birthday it is time you knew all the facts. Before you were born Aegeus put his sword and his sandal under the great boulder that you see yonder. When you are strong enough to do so, you are to lift the boulder and take the sword and sandal to him as evidence of your identity. He will then welcome you and you will be his heir.

Theseus: [jumping up] Mother, I am sixteen now. I am old enough and certainly strong enough to lift that boulder. I will do it now. [exits left]

Aethra: [to the audience] I hope I have not told him all this too soon. If he is able to move that boulder, he will leave us, and he is so young. He does not know how hard and dangerous life can be. His grandfather, the respected king of Troezen, and I will sorely miss him.

Grandfather: [enters from left] Where is Theseus? I wish to speak to him about the hunting trip we are going to make together.

Aethra: Father, I told Theseus about the boulder. He ran out the door so that he could immediately move it.

Grandfather: That boy is as strong as his cousin, Hercules, but of course he is young. When he reaches manhood he could be even stronger. Still, there is no doubt that he will move it today.

Aethra: Dear father, we will miss him so. I wish I had waited to tell him.

Grandfather: It is only right that you told him, but we will both be saddened by his departure.

Theseus: [entering from right carrying sandal and sword] Mother and Grandfather, I have here the sword and sandal of my father. I must go to Athens immediately. I hear there are many bandits who bother travelers between here and Athens. I am strong so I'll take care of them.

Grandfather: No, no! You must go by ship. It is a short journey across the Saronic Gulf and it will be a safer trip. If you travel as you say, you could be killed. I will have a ship made ready for you.

Theseus: No, dear Grandfather. Although I deeply respect you, I must now act as I see fit. My cousin, Hercules, would never shun such a trip.

Grandfather: There you go, comparing yourself with your cousin. We all know you are as brave as your cousin. And you shall prove it someday, but now you are still so young. Give yourself a chance. No one doubts your courage.

Theseus: Grandfather and Mother, have no fear. I am healthy and I am in good condition. You will be proud of me.

[curtain]

Act II. Manhood.

SCENE 1. A room in palace of Aegeus, king of Athens.

Medea is present with her son Medus.

[curtain]

Medea: I know that the young man who arrived here the other day is the son of Aegeus, but the king does not know it.

Medus: Mother, the king is really interested in this youth, who by the way is named Theseus. The story of his exploits reached Athens before he did. Without help he wiped out some vicious monsters that were spoiling the travel between cities. Theseus has become very popular with the people of Athens. He is considered a hero.

Medea: And that has the king worried. It seems that he is afraid that because Theseus is so popular the people will want to make him king.

Medus: But Mother, you can use your powers to see that this doesn't happen.

Medea: [taps her chin with her hand] You are right! I certainly will do my best. I will mix a poison for him. The king is giving a dinner for him tonight and so this very night he can be given the potion. I have already spoken to Aegeus, and he too wants Theseus destroyed.

Medus: Mother, how did you get the old king to agree to that?

Medea: It really wasn't so difficult. You know that the fifty sons of the king's half-brother are trying to make one of them king, so all I had to do was convince Aegeus that Theseus was going to help the nephews overthrow him. In fact, it was simple. Aegeus goes into a rage whenever the sons of his half-brother are even mentioned.

Medus: Mother, I know you want the crown for me. But just in case your plan goes awry, do you have your winged chariot ready? We may have to make a hasty exit.

Medea: Put your thoughts at ease. Come, let us go down to the dinner.

[curtain]

SCENE 2. Royal dining hall.

King Aegeus and Medea are speaking.

[curtain]

Aegeus: So we are ready for the great feast. I am anxious to meet the young man.

Medea: [with malice] Yes, here he comes, I will offer him a refreshing cup of wine.

Aegeus: So be it. He certainly made a name for himself.

Medea: Here he comes. Look at the confident way in which he strides. Why all of Athens adores him. I think they would make him king.

Aegeus: Well, we'll put an end to such thinking.

Theseus: [presenting himself to the king] Good King Aegeus, it is with happiness that I accept your invitation to dinner.

Aegeus: Come then, let us begin. I wish to hear firsthand of all your exploits.

Medea: [turns sideways so that Theseus does not see her pour poison into the cup that she is about to give him] Theseus, may this refresh you.

Theseus: Thank you for your kindness. [he draws the sword to show his father]

Aegeus: [recognizing sword, leaps across stage and knocks cup out of Theseus' hand] My son! My own son!

Medea: [to Medus] Come quickly, follow me. Our chariot is ready, as you so aptly suggested. [exits right]

Theseus: What is all this commotion? I know you recognize me for you called me "son." But why did you come at me with such haste and knock the cup out of my hand?

Aegeus: This is a long story. Until I saw the sword, I did not know you to be my son. Rather I thought you a very strong young man who might help my nephews take over the crown. I should not have listened to Medea. But I did. I'll explain in detail later. Let us now enjoy the feast in your honor and I will present you to the people of Athens as my rightful heir.

Theseus: As you wish, dear father.

[dim lights for twenty seconds; Aegeus and Theseus are both seated on a bench, stage left, in front of the open curtain]

Aegeus: And so beloved son, I am glad that you pulled my sword when you did. My joy in having you with me is great indeed. How is your mother and her father, the respected king of Troezen?

Theseus: My mother is well. She keeps herself busy, especially taking care of my grandfather because he is growing old now. He knew that I would want to come to you as soon as I was able and did everything to help me get ready. He was much against my traveling by land because he feared for my safety. By now he knows I arrived here and that truly I am as strong or hopefully stronger than my cousin, Hercules.

Aegeus: So you compete with your cousin. That is natural. Brother competes with brother, cousin with cousin. I am pleased to have you as my son.

Theseus: Father, I heard about King Minos and the tribute in human blood that you must regularly pay. It was a sad day that his son, Androgeus, was killed by a dangerous bull while visiting here. But, still it is a very harsh punishment that King Minos meted out. In a month, the seven youths and seven maidens that King Minos demands be sent to him every nine years, will be leaving for Crete. The suffering demanded of these innocent young people is too horrible to contemplate. I want to go with them. In fact, I want to take the place of one of the youths, and Father, I will fell the Minotaur before we can become his fodder.

Aegeus: [quickly interrupting] No, my son. I forbid it. Only now have you come into my life. Do not leave it so soon. No one can overcome the Minotaur, the monster with a bull's body and a human head.

Theseus: Yes, Father, I can do so. I will outwit him and I will get out of the maze. My strength is great but besides this I will use my brain and figure a way out. In fact, before I even go into the labyrinth, I will have a plan. You'll see.

Aegeus: I can see you are determined. I greatly admire your spirit.

Theseus: When the ship sails with the human tribute the flags will be black. When you see the ship again, sailing brightly into the port, we will be flying white flags which will be a signal to you that I have succeeded and that all is well.

Aegeus: May the gods protect you.

[curtain]

Act III. The proving grounds.

SCENE 1. Room in the palace of King Minos of Crete.

Ariadne, daughter of King Minos, and Daedalus, architect of the labyrinth, are talking to each other.

[curtain]

Daedalus: But Princess Ariadne, you are asking the impossible of me. How can I possibly tell you the secrets of the labyrinth and how Theseus can escape?

Ariadne: But if you saw Theseus yourself, you could not knowingly send him to his death. I saw him with the other youths and maidens when they were marching down the street on the way from the ship. They are to be taken into the maze and abandoned there until the Minotaur is hungry at which time he will devour them. It is too cruel, too inhumane to do this.

Daedalus: But you've never said anything before?

Ariadne: Nine years ago I was too young to have had it make an impression. This time I saw the handsome, courageous Theseus and I truly love him. Please Daedalus, help me.

Daedalus: But what if your father the king were to find out that I helped you in this endeavor?

Ariadne: Trust me. I too, would be in grave danger if he were to find out my plot. Help me, and I will forever remain silent.

Daedalus: My wits are confused by this whole thing, but my heart seems clear. Come listen carefully. [Ariadne draws closer to Daedalus]

[curtain]

SCENE 2: Same as scene 1, a few hours later.

Ariadne is speaking to Theseus. Both are standing at stage center.

[curtain]

Ariadne: And so I sent for you because I have news for you, very important news.

Theseus: Princess Ariadne, this is an honor I did not expect. I was shocked when I was summoned to the palace. Tell me is my father ill?

Ariadne: No, I saw you in the march from the ship and my heart leaped in distress at your plight. Immediately I spoke to Daedalus, the architect of the infamous labyrinth. He has told me how you can escape from the labyrinth, something no one has ever been able to do.

Theseus: Tell me, Ariadne, what must I do?

Ariadne: Theseus, I will be direct. I fell in love with you. My heart leaped in my body when I saw you for the first time. If I tell you how to get out of the labyrinth, will you take me back to Athens with you and make me your wife?

Theseus: Need you ask? Of course, and believe me, it will not be a difficult assignment.

Ariadne: Then we must make plans. [she goes over to table at right and takes a ball of thread in her hand] This, sweet Theseus, is the answer.

Theseus: [looking shocked] But how can this ball of thread be of help?

Ariadne: It is really quite simple. When you enter the labyrinth fasten the end of the thread to the inside of the door. As you continue walking into the labyrinth, allow the thread to unwind. When you want to leave the labyrinth, just follow the thread and come out. I will be waiting for you.

Theseus: I do believe it will work. [pause] Yes! It will work. I will be the first one to go into the maze. I will find the Minotaur and slay him before he finds me. Ariadne, you will never regret this. I will be good to you. We will return to Athens in glory and you will be my queen when I inherit the throne.

[curtain]

SCENE 3: Aboard ship on the way back to Athens.

The black flags are still flying. Theseus is talking to Ariadne and two crewmen.

[curtain]

Theseus: It really wasn't hard. I ...

Crewman #1: [interrupting] Theseus, come now, you slew the dreaded Minotaur. It couldn't have been easy.

Theseus: Let us put it this way. I have had harder tasks. But true, it did take some exertion and I was very tired, but happily tired when I finished. I slowly sneaked around in the labyrinth and finally found him asleep. Leaping upon him I grabbed him by the horns and bashed his head on the rocks. He awakened and only shock and horror could describe his countenance.

Ariadne: Theseus, I do indeed want to hear every detail. Nothing is too small for my ear, but now I feel ill. I can hardly stand up.

Theseus: [taking her hand] Ariadne, I do believe you are seasick. We will put in at the very next isle. We are due to pass Naxos within a short time.

Crewman #2: Do you want me to give the order to slacken our speed and get ready to drop anchor when we approach Naxos?

Theseus: Yes, this is good. Ariadne needs to rest awhile. I will accompany her to the shore and then return to the ship for some work that I must do.

[dim lights for a few seconds]

Theseus: Ariadne and two maids are resting. We shall stay at anchor for a few hours and then I will return to shore for them.

Crewman #1: Royal lord, we are drifting. The anchor has broken loose and the winds are beginning to blow. We are in for a great storm. I fear we will be blown far out to sea.

Theseus: I'll be at the helm.

[thunder, lightning, roar of the ocean]

Theseus: [stands downstage center, facing audience] The storm took us way off course. For a number of days we wandered and finally were able to maneuver our way back to Naxos. There my heart died, for Ariadne, the dear girl that loved me and literally saved me from endless wandering in the labyrinth, was dead. We headed for home but in my grief I failed to hoist the white flags. This spelled doom for my father, Aegeus. He saw the black flags still flying and took this to mean that I did not escape from the Minotaur. He threw himself down a steep cliff and was killed.

[curtain]

Act IV. The leader.

SCENE 1. A room in the Athenian palace.

Present are Theseus, Aethra, and an aide.

[curtain]

Theseus: Mother, I can not begin to tell you how happy I am that you have come to live with me. All Athenians rejoice in my good fortune.

Aethra: Son, I thought at first it would be difficult to leave Troezen, the land where I spent all my life until now. Being with you has made the difference. I scarcely think of Troezen at all. You have so many interesting things going on at all times and I've met so many people that love me because they love you.

Theseus: Mother, I am sure they love you for yourself. You are always gracious and warm to them.

Aethra: I can see that you are a good king, a wise and thoughtful king. Your people look to you for guidance.

Theseus: I do want to guide them but not to rule them. I do not wish to be a king who tells people what to do. I want the government to be the people, the people making the decisions by their vote.

Man #1: Athens will be a happy and prosperous city, a true democratic society.

Man #2: [entering from left] Theseus, what about Adrastus who came from Argos today? What does he want? He seemed so anxious.

Theseus: Of course we didn't discuss it. I put him at his ease and commented that he must be tired after his trip. After we feast this evening, I will ask him what brings him to Athens.

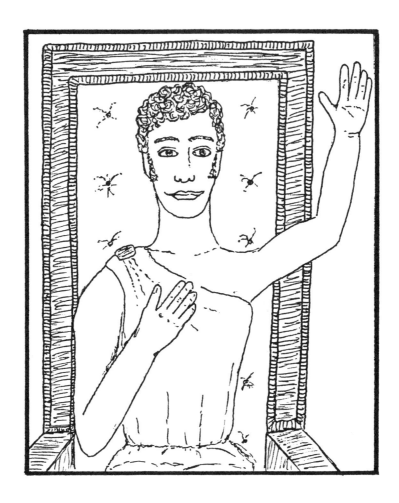

Man #2: But surely he has come about the problem in Thebes. My heart aches for all those involved. I hear that it was a fearful struggle. Of the seven rulers who beseiged Thebes, Adrastus was the only survivor. He is distraught.

Theseus: We shall soon enough know what brings him to Athens. More than likely he wants assistance of some kind. But we shall see.

[dim lights for twenty seconds]

Adrastus: The dinner was delicious and the company excellent. But let me get to the serious business at hand. I come asking you to prevail on the Thebans to act in a just manner. Our slain leaders cannot find peace in the Underworld unless they have a proper burial and the Thebans will not allow us to bury them.

Theseus: Come now. You know better than to ask me. I do not help those who start a war.

Aethra: [walking toward Theseus] Since coming to make my home with you I have noticed a wonderful spirit in this city. Son, may I speak for your honor and for Athens?

Theseus: So be it. [listens intently]

Aethra: You are a courageous man. You are a just man. So you cannot stand by and watch others do an injustice to fellow human beings. I am talking about human rights.

Theseus: I have heard words of wisdom from you, my honored mother. I agree with you but I cannot act on my own. I will call the citizens in assembly. If they agree I will take a stand. [exits left]

[characters freeze on the stage and lights are dimmed; after twenty seconds, lights go up; characters come alive]

Theseus: [entering from left] The assembly has voted to tell the Thebans that Athens wishes to be a good neighbor, but that they cannot stand by and see a great wrong done. This means that we will personally go and bury the dead.

[curtain]

Act V. The friend.

Theseus and Pirithous are standing in front of the curtain to the right.

[curtain]

Narrator: In the meantime, Pirithous, a young ruler from the north had heard many tales about Theseus and wanted very much to meet him. So he did it the simple way. He decided to ride south into the area east of Athens where Theseus kept his herds of beautiful cattle. He would steal the cattle. This way he would certainly meet Theseus.

Theseus: Pirithous, this was a very rash act on your part. I cannot imagine what possessed you. I have heard tales of your foolhardiness, but trying to steal my cattle is the end.

Pirithous: I wanted to get to know you. I figured if I stole your prized cattle you would come after me. And certainly this would be an opportunity for me to observe you. [pause] Actually I wanted to see if you are as great a hero as you are reported to be.

Theseus: And to what conclusion did you come?

Pirithous: You have more valor than could be expected of any man. I did steal your cattle. [extending his hand] I submit to any penalty you impose. You be the judge.

Theseus: [obviously pleased, says with a smile] All I want is for you to be my brother-in-arms. Come. We will take a solemn oath of undying friendship. I, Theseus, do solemnly swear that Pirithous will always be my friend and I will abide by the laws of friendship.

Pirithous: I do solemnly swear that Theseus will always be my friend and I will abide by the laws of friendship.

[curtain]

SCENE 1. Afternoon in Theseus's palace.

Enter Theseus, followed by Pirithous.

Pirithous: I really think it will be a wonderful experience. A voyage through the straits and into the Euxine Sea always offers a challenge. Come with me.

Theseus: I just might do that. I really haven't had a good adventure since I accompanied Hercules when he visited the Amazons.

Pirithous: So it is settled then. You will come.

Theseus: Yes, count me in.

Pirithous: This is my plan. We shall sail, going up the coast and finally cutting across the open sea, stopping at various islands. When finally in the Euxine Sea we shall stay close to the southern shore watching for landmarks that will tell us that we are approaching the Amazon territory.

Theseus: There is one thing I do remember. Those Amazons are really sharp shooters with the arrows. Right from shore they can kill men aboard ship. They are uncanny. I would suggest that when we get close to the shores that we lash our shields together to make a bulwark on one side of the ship.

Pirithous: Great idea.

Theseus: I remember the queen from the expedition with Hercules. She was beautiful, her tunic laced with gold, her hair flowing gently in the breeze. She was everything, splendid to behold, intelligent, gracious, and a warrior.

Pirithous: You sound as if she really means something to you. Are you in love, Theseus?

Theseus: Come now, it has been ages since I have seen her. Still, she is hard to forget.

Pirithous: Obviously, you have not forgotten her. Theseus, you have never married. Why don't you propose marriage to this queen?

Theseus: I can see you don't understand the Amazons. I don't propose to Antiope, for that is her name. A man doesn't propose to an Amazon woman. The Amazon selects whom she wishes.

Pirithous: Well, if I were you I would think of some way to get around this. Perhaps ask your oracle about it.

Theseus: Forget Antiope for now. What do we need to get ready for this trip? When shall we leave? Who shall we take with us?

Pirithous: Perhaps we could send out heralds announcing our voyage. Many young men will be happy for the opportunity. Now to make our plans. There is much to be done. [Theseus and Pirithous get busy at a table with charts and maps]

[curtain]

SCENE 2. Palace in Athens.

Enter Theseus and Antiope, talking earnestly.

Narrator: Time passed. Theseus and Pirithous took this voyage. And yes, Antiope did select Theseus. Some say that he captured her when she brought presents aboard the ship. Some say otherwise. Whatever, if she was captured, she was a willing prisoner and readily accompanied Theseus to Athens. Her sisters were simply outraged and although it took a long time, they got a band together to follow her all the way to Athens. They crossed the icy Bosphorus and came down through Thrace and Thessaly. Athens was at war.

[curtain]

Theseus: Antiope, my dear, I know that it is very difficult for you to take arms against your own sisters. This is a very sad time for both of us.

Antiope: I worry so about our son, Hippolytos. It is not good for him to see all this bloodshed. And for what purpose?

Theseus: Your sisters are adamant. They traveled hundreds and hundreds of miles and faced all kinds of adverse conditions, including bad weather and hostile people. A messenger says that if you will return with them, all hostilities will cease.

Antiope: But that would mean that you and I would have to part. I will not leave you. It is true that my sisters and I ruled the Amazon country together, but that does not mean that the country cannot continue without me. My sisters are not seeing clearly. And our son needs his mother. And I need you.

Theseus: And I need you, dear Antiope. The problem is of course that your sisters have Ares, the god of war, on their side. [adviser enters from left]

Adviser: I overheard what you just said. I must say that there is more to this. If the Amazons defeat us, they will have a marvelous victory. Not only will they claim Antiope, but they will control western civilization as well. Even though we are the most formidable foes they have ever had, they are determined. But all is quiet right now.

Theseus: There is a truce for the moment to give us all time to bury the dead.

Adviser: We would be wise to get word to all Athenians to tighten their belts. We must ration all food.

Theseus: Absolutely. Take care of this by proclamation.

Narrator: The Athenians did win the war. It was the first time ever that they had seen their city besieged. The fighting was bloody and hard, the Amazon's shrieking battle cries indeed terrifying. The war was costly in human life. At its end, Antiope lay dead, felled by an arrow from an Amazon. Theseus went into mourning.

[curtain]

Act VI. The Underworld.

SCENE 1. Darkened passageway.

Theseus and Pirithous are walking along the front of a darkened stage.

[curtain]

Narrator: Mourning didn't last forever. For his next marriage, Theseus chose Phaedra, sister of Ariadne and second daughter of Minos, the king of Crete. Things didn't work out too well, because Hippolytos, now a young man, was the subject of grave concern for Phaedra. Phaedra became madly in love with Hippolytos. It all ended with

Hippolytos ignoring Phaedra, Phaedra killing herself, and Theseus calling down a curse on his son. In the meantime, Pirithous, that old friend of Theseus, was dreaming up a new adventure. He convinced Theseus, and really much against Theseus's will, that Theseus should accompany him on a dangerous mission to the Underworld. Theseus would have to pay for this undying friendship.

Enter Pirithous, followed by Theseus.

Pirithous: Step carefully here. Coming in this back door to the Underworld saves us a good deal of trouble, such as dealing with Cerberus, the three-headed dog, and Charon, the ferryman. But it does take a little more effort.

Theseus: How much longer do we have to travel?

Pirithous: Well you know that I have never been here myself, but I suspect it won't be too much longer.

Theseus: Let us rest here a moment. [sits down] Now what do you propose to tell Hades?

Pirithous: [sitting down] I decided to be open and honest about it. I want to take Persephone back with me. I wish to have her as my wife.

Theseus: This is ludicrous. Are you crazy? You do come up with the wildest schemes. He will never give you permission for this. Since he doesn't know how to laugh, I won't say that he will laugh at you, but he certainly will be scornful.

Pirithous: Would you suggest that I just snatch Persephone?

Theseus: I suggest that you abandon the whole foolhardy idea.

Pirithous: I can see you are in no mood for adventure. We've rested enough. Come along. [the two rise; lights become less dim, but not bright; Theseus and Pirithous back onto the stage; Hades sits at stage right]

Hades: What brings you two fellows here? This is most unusual.

Pirithous: We are paying a social call.

Hades: Come now, people don't pay me social calls. I don't understand this. Why didn't Charon notify me that he ferried you across the river? And what happened to Cerberus?

Theseus: We came in the back way. It sure was longer but then we didn't have to bother with Cerberus and Charon.

Pirithous: When we have rested we will lay bare our souls and ask your advice.

Hades: Good fellows, please be seated. [the two sit on two chairs and horrified expressions come over their faces] So now you are seated forever. Enjoy! You will sit and think of your sins. I know very well why you came here Pirithous. Why are you so naive? This is a new dimension in your personality that I had not noticed before. You will have plenty of time to think.

Narrator: Four years passed. Four long years in which Theseus and Pirithous sat glued to the chairs. Certainly, this gave them plenty of time to think of their sins.

[Hercules enters from left]

Hades: Everytime I turn around it seems there is a new invasion and they aren't all souls. Now what do you want?

Hercules: I came here on another mission but while here I thought I would discuss with you the problems of my cousin, Theseus, and of course of his friend, Pirithous.

Hades: There is no problem. They are here and that is all there is to it.

Hercules: I would like to take them back to the upper world with me.

Hades: Certainly, just help them to their feet and take them.

Hercules: [to Theseus] Come dear cousin. It is over. Give me your hands. [with a terrific tug, he pulls Theseus lose] Now you are free.

Theseus: My cousin, dear cousin. May the gods bless you. But please help my friend.

Hercules: [to Pirithous] Give me your hands. [he tugs and tugs] It is impossible. We shall have to leave without him.

Theseus: [embraces Pirithous] My heart is sorrowing for you …

Hades: [interrupting] Get out of here now, before I change my mind.

Narrator: Theseus had his problems when he got back to Athens. He decided to travel to Crete but he was blown off course and ended up on the island of Scyros. If Theseus died as the result of treachery, or accidentally or because of illness we do not know. But he really died this time. His entry into the Underworld was without fanfare and this time he stayed.

[curtain]

TEACHERS' NOTES

1. Using transparency number 1, have the students tell you what part of the world they see. Write on the transparency: Southern Europe, Near East, North Africa, and the Mediterranean Sea. Give the students a map and have them lightly color in the water area with a blue pencil. Using transparency number 4, have them locate Crete, Taenarus, Troezen, Athens, Naxos, Bosphorus, and Euxine Sea. All these places are important to the play.

2. Some mythologists say that Theseus deliberately abandoned Ariadne, and that Dionysus rescued her and eventually married her.[1] Others say that the whole affair was accidental due to an unexpected storm.

3. Looking at Theseus as a young man and in the early adult years, he seemed courageous, generous, and a man who believed in justice. As the years went on it would seem that his judgment grew poor. Perhaps it was his association with Pirithous, who certainly didn't think things through.

Theseus Transparency Master no. 4

VOCABULARY

adamant. unyielding; not giving in easily, firm

adverse. acting against someone or something

aptly. likely or almost certain

awry. wrong, amiss

beseige. to surround an area with soldiers and keep it under attack so as to force a surrender

bulwark. a wall for defending against an enemy

contemplate. to think about carefully

democratic. treating people of all classes in same way

dimension. size or importance

endeavor. to try hard, make an effort

exploits. daring acts, bold deeds

fodder. a coarse food for cattle, horses, etc.

formidable. hard to do or take care of

infamous. very bad, wicked

inhumane. cruel, heartless

malice. ill will, spite

maze. series of winding passages having many dead ends and seeming not to have an outlet

totalitarian. a government where all but one party is outlawed

tribute. forced payment

ACTIVITIES

1. Make a map of Theseus's various journeys.

2. Prepare an original oratory on human rights. Use Theseus and his desire for human rights as an example. Tie in with modern examples.

3. Pretend you are Theseus. Keep a diary for a week in one of the following periods: as a youth in Troezen; the week he was united with his father, King Aegeus; on board ship after killing the Minotaur.

4. Write a letter from Theseus to Aethra after arriving in Athens for the first time, or write from Aethra to Theseus just after Theseus left Troezen.

5. Write an essay in which you chronicle the events of Theseus's life.

DISCUSSION QUESTIONS

Name_____

The Greatest Athenian Act I

1. What secret did Theseus's mother tell him on his sixteenth birthday?

2. What conflict surfaced between Theseus and his grandfather?

3. Theseus feels that strength and courage are the most important virtues in life. What do you think?

4. How would Theseus's life have been different had he been unable to lift the boulder?

5. What kind of relationship do you think Theseus had with his grandfather?

6. Was Aethra right or wrong in withholding the truth about his father?

7. Were you happy that Theseus was able to lift the boulder. Why or why not?

8. Using examples write a paragraph about the maturity of Theseus. Perhaps your topic sentence could be: "Theseus shows signs of maturity in act I."

Name_____

The Greatest Athenian Act II

1. What does Medus report that Theseus did on the way to Athens?

2. Why did Medea wish to poison Theseus?

3. Why did King Aegeus go along with Medea's plan?

4. What kind of powers do you think Medea has?

5. Some stories say that Medea escaped Athens in a chariot drawn by serpents. Which do you think would provide the quickest getaway? Why?

6. Theseus said, "By now, my grandfather knows that I arrived here." How do you think the king of Troezen received the news?

7. What do you predict will happen to Theseus when he goes with young Athenians to Crete?

8. Research Periphetes, Sinis, Sciron, Cerycon, and Procrustus.

Name_____

The Greatest Athenian Act III

1. Why did Ariadne summon Daedalus to the palace?

2. In what order did these events occur?

    (   )   Ariadne tells Daedalus that she also would be in danger.

    (   )   Ariadne goes ashore to rest.

    (   )   Theseus forgets to raise white flag.

    (   )   Daedalus gives Ariadne ball of thread.

    (   )   King Aegeus throws himself off cliff.

    (   )   Crewman says anchor has broken loose.

    (   )   Ariadne gives Theseus a ball of thread.

    (   )   Theseus slays the Minotaur.

3. Ariadne proposed marriage to Theseus. How do you feel about this approach?

4. What conflict did helping Theseus present to Ariadne? Have you ever had a similar conflict? Explain.

5. Do you think Ariadne made a right decision? Why or why not?

6. What would have happened to Theseus if Ariadne had not come to his aid?

7. What might have King Minos done if Daedalus reported Ariadne's treachery?

8. Write a paragraph comparing Ariadne in *The Great Athenian* and Medea in *The Golden Fleece*. The topic sentence might be "Ariadne and Medea were alike in many ways."

Name_____

The Greatest Athenian Act IV

1. What kind of government does Theseus want to have in Athens?

2. Why is the visitor upset because the Thebans refuse burial to six leaders who died in the war against Thebes?

3. Why does Aethra say, "Theseus cannot stand by and watch an injustice done"?

4. What do you think would have happened if the assembly voted not to interfere with the Thebans?

5. If Theseus were alive today would he be a head of state in a democratic or totalitarian society? Why?

6. How did Theseus abide by the law of hospitality?

7. What kind of a relationship do you think Theseus has with his mother?

8. First research the meanings of totalitarian and democratic and then write a paragraph in which you contrast a democratic government and a totalitarian government. Your paragraph might start: "A democratic government and a totalitarian government differ in several important ways."

Name_____

The Greatest Athenian Act **V**

1. Why does Pirithous try to steal Theseus's cattle?

2. Why did Theseus not get angry at Pirithous?

3. Do you think there is a possibility that Theseus will regret the oath of friendship?

4. How would you compare Ariadne and Antiope in their attitude toward marriage and men?

5. How might Theseus's life have been different had he never met Pirithous?

6. From what you read here about the Amazons' attack on Athens, how did their type war differ from ours?

7. Why did Theseus suggest they fasten their shields together to form a bulwark?

8. Research the Amazons.

Name_____

The Greatest Athenian **Act VI**

1. How do you feel about Theseus taking the part of Phaedra and putting a curse on his own son? Hou could this have been handled differently? Do these types of situations arise in families today?

2. Where did Pirithous ask Theseus to accompany him?

3. Do you think Theseus regretted his oath of undying friendship to Pirithous? Why or why not?

4. Name the three foolhardy things that Pirithous did in this play.

5. Do you think Theseus made a right decision in accompanying his friend to the Underworld?

6. Has someone ever tried to talk you into doing something you knew was not right for you? If so, how did you handle it?

7. What adjectives would you use to describe:

   Theseus

   Pirithous

   Hercules

   Hades

8. Write a paragraph using examples on the demands of friendship enlarging your topic sentence. Your topic sentence might be: "Being a good friend places certain demands on a person."

TESTS

Name_____

The Greatest Athenian Test Yourself

Choose from the list below and fill in the blanks.

Amazons	Hippolytos	Ariadne	Minotaur
Scyros	Theseus	Daedalus	Saronic
Phaedra	Medea	Androgeus	Hercules
Antiope	Aethra	Medus	Aegeus
Euxine Sea	Pirithous	Crete	King of Troezen

1. _____Theseus retired here.

2. _____Amazons lived on southern coast.

3. _____He and Theseus vowed eternal friendship.

4. _____Architect of the labyrinth.

5. _____She was left on Naxos.

6. _____Half man and half bull.

7. _____Son of King Minos who was killed.

8. _____Greatest Athenian hero.

9. _____Gulf between Troezen and Athens.

10. _____She learned from Hecate.

11. _____Strong cousin of Theseus.

12. _____Grandfather of Theseus.

13. _____Mother of Theseus.

14. _____Father of Theseus.

15. _____Son of Medea.

16. _____Labyrinth located here.

17. _____Warrior women.

18. _____Theseus abducted her and married her.

19. _____Second daughter of King Minos.

20. _____Son of Antiope.

Name_____

The Greatest Athenian **Final Test**

Choose the correct answer and mark the corresponding letter in the parentheses.

( )   1.   Theseus's wife Antiope was: (a) an Amazon (b) an Ithacan (c) Athenian.

( )   2.   When Theseus left Athens for the last time he took refuge in: (a) Sparta (b) Seriphos (c) Scyros.

( )   3.   Ariadne was left on the island of: (a) Siphnos (b) Chios (c) Naxos.

( )   4.   The mother of Theseus was: (a) Aethra (b) Ariadne (c) Antiope.

( )   5.   Androgeus was the son of: (a) Pittheus (b) Minos (c) Medus.

( )   6.   The Minotaur was: (a) half man and half bull (b) half man and half horse (c) half man and half cow.

( )   7.   Theseus was the greatest hero of: (a) Crete (b) Sparta (c) Athens.

( )   8.   The warrior women who lived on the southeastern shore of the Euxine Sea were: (a) Amazons (b) Thessalians (c) Thracians.

( )   9.   The labyrinth was a famous: (a) jungle (b) maze (c) coliseum.

( )   10.   Medea was: (a) an enchantress (b) witch (c) goddess in disguise.

( )   11.   Theseus was born in: (a) Troezen (b) Athens (c) Nemea.

( )   12.   When asked by Pirithous to accompany him to the Underworld, Theseus was: (a) delighted (b) excited (c) unhappy.

( )   13.   Theseus and Pirithous entered the Underworld by: (a) crossing the ferry with Charon (b) leaping over gate protected by Cerberus (c) going in a back door from a cave in Taenarus.

( )   14.   Theseus stayed with the Amazons: (a) one year (b) three years (c) no time at all.

( )   15.   The Thebans refused: (a) to bury dead leaders (b) to salute the flag of Athens (c) to allow refugees to enter.

( )   16.   Aethra pleaded with Theseus to consider: (a) loyalty (b) human rights (c) honesty.

( )   17.   When Theseus first met Pirithous, Pirithous was: (a) trying to steal Theseus's cattle (b) at a wedding (c) trying to steal sheep.

( )   18.   After the death of Antiope, Theseus married: (a) Medea (b) Phaedra (c) Danae.

( )   19.   Which of the following was used to help Theseus escape the labyrinth: (a) a ball of yarn (b) a ball of thread (c) a ball of wire.

( )   20.   Minos was the king of: (a) Crete (b) Cyprus (c) Lemnos.

THE GREATEST ATHENIAN CROSSWORD PUZZLE CLUES

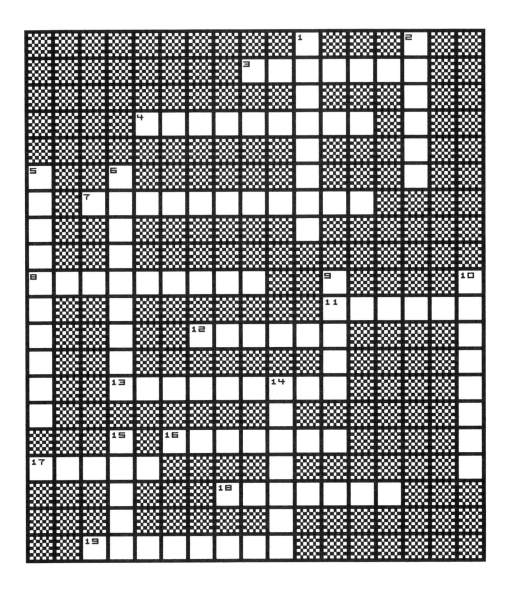

Across

3. She asked Theseus to take her with him
4. King of North Thessaly
7. Gulf separating Troezen from Athens
8. Killed by bull while visiting Athens
11. Another name for Black Sea
12. Theseus used this to escape from labyrinth
13. Son of Antiope and Theseus
16. Son of Aegeus of Athens
17. King of the Underworld
18. Sharpshooters with arrows
19. Architect of labyrinth

Down

1. Half man and half bull
2. Mother of Theseus
5. Ruler of Athens
6. Housed the Minotaur
9. The son of Medea
10. Three-headed dog
14. They refused to bury the dead leaders
15. Wife of Aegeus who tried to poison Theseus

NOTES

1. H. J. Rose, *A Handbook of Mythology* (New York: Dutton, 1959), 265.

Perseus

THE PLAY

Cast of Characters
In Order of Appearance

Dictys, a fisherman
Danaë, daughter of King Acrisius of Argolis
Polydectes, king of Seriphos
Servant, court of Polydectes
Perseus, son of Danaë
Athena, goddess of wisdom
Hermes, messenger of Zeus
Deino, one of the Gray Sisters
Enyo, one of the Gray Sisters
Pemphredo, one of the Gray Sisters
Andromeda, daughter of King Cepheus
Cepheus, king of Ethiopia
Cassiopeia, mother of Andromeda
Phineus, suitor of Andromeda
Adviser, court of Polydectes

Act I. A boy.

SCENE 1. A beach on the shores of Seriphos.

Narrator: A fisherman, weary from hauling his nets, and even more tired from fighting the elements all day, sat for a moment on the rocky beach of Seriphos. His thoughts were of his rather mean-spirited brother, who was actually the king of this island. His brother was so different, wealthy and greedy, while he was on the poor side but ready to share anything. His thoughts were interrupted when he noticed a very large box, more like a casket, being bounced around in the surf. Dictys, the fisherman, was quick to act. [when the curtain opens, the box is safely on shore]

[curtain]

Dictys:	[to Danaë who is sitting on box holding a baby] What powers could have brought you here? It is a wonder you are alive. Stretch out on this blanket. [spreads blanket on sand]
Danaë:	Thank you, thank you. I am indeed worn out.
Dictys:	What put you in this terrible situation? But wait, do not answer me. I will get some water out of my goat-skin bag so that you might be refreshed. [she sits and drinks and gives the baby some water] Please eat some of this delicious fruit and freshly baked bread. [leans over and takes infant from Danaë] Come little fellow, give your mother a chance to renew her strength.
Danaë:	Thank you, kind sir, you are most hospitable. Let me tell you who I am. My name is Danaë and I am the daughter of King Acrisius of Argolis. It is strange that I should be sitting here on this beach. The gods must be with me or I would not have survived. I do not like to put the blame on my own father for this circumstance in which I find myself, but there is no other one responsible.
Dictys:	Your father? How could this be? He is a respected man.
Danaë:	Yes, he is, but he lives in fear.
Dictys:	Tell me why. Just why does your powerful father live in fear?
Danaë:	One time an oracle told him that he must beware of a grandson. The oracle said that he would never have a son of his own and that one day a grandson would rise up and kill him. When my son was born he was devastated. I tried to explain that my son is the son of Zeus but he would not listen to me. Rather than kill little Perseus, he put us both in this box hoping that we would then be out of his life. [weeping]
Dictys:	Dry those tears. You will come home with me. Tomorrow I will take you to my brother, King Polydectes of Seriphos, for that is the name of this island, and I will implore his help for you.

[curtain]

SCENE 2. A room in the palace of King Polydectes.

Enter King Polydectes and servant.

[curtain]

Narrator:	In the meantime Dictys took Danaë and her baby home where his wife welcomed them both. The next day he took Danaë and the baby to his brother's palace.

Servant: Your highness, your brother is here to see you.

King: [annoyed] What does Dictys want? He should know better than to come here without an invitation.

Servant: He has a young woman and a baby with him, your highness.

King: Very well, show him in. [servant exits left] My brother will never amount to anything. It is a pity that I must be bothered with his problems. I wonder what kind of a fix he is in now?

Servant: [enters from left followed by Dictys, Danaë, and the baby] Your brother, sir.

King: Yes, yes. Come in Dictys. And who might this young lady be? [face brightens]

Danaë: I can speak for myself. I am Danaë, daughter of King Acrisius of Argolis, and this is my son. My father put us in a box and set us in the sea. Please don't think poorly of my father. He did what he had to do, as the oracle told him that one day a grandson would kill him. For his own protection and the protection of his crown, he put us out to sea. He did not want to kill the baby and that speaks well for him. I pray that you will see fit to help us.

King: What is the little fellow's name?

Danaë: Perseus.

King: A very nice name. My dear, I will be happy to help you. You must live here with me and I will bring up Perseus, and give him knowledge in all the duties of what some day might be his state of life.

Dictys: Brother of mine, I wish that Danaë will live with my wife and myself. She has agreed to do so.

King: [to Danaë] Is this what you wish?

Danaë: You are both kind, but yes, I wish to live with Dictys. It was he who found us.

King: As you wish, but I will keep Perseus here. You will of course visit him regularly.

[curtain]

Act II. Adventure.

SCENE 1. Palace of King Polydectes, eighteen years later.

Polydectes and Perseus are present.

[curtain]

King:	Well Perseus, you are now a man. I invite you to the festivities in honor of my intended bride, Princess Hippodameia. All the invited guests have been asked to bring a horse as a gift. Hippodameia loves horses, you know. Surely that isn't too much to ask.
Perseus:	From me it is too much. I have nothing that I can truly call my own. You have been good to me but I have always suspected it was because you really like my mother and would like to make her queen.
King:	How you talk! Where do you get such ideas?
Perseus:	So you mean you are really not interested in my mother?
King:	No, I am not. Trust me. But about the present for my intended ...
Perseus:	[interrupting] Ask anything of me. I'll do anything for you, even get the Gorgon's head for you, but I cannot afford a horse.
King:	Fantastic idea! The Gorgon's head. I've long wanted it. Do it.
Perseus:	You really do want the Gorgon's head. I've always known that. And you think that I can do it?
King:	You are strong and young. I know that you will be successful.
Perseus:	It would be better not to tell my mother until after I have left. She will worry and try to stop me. First I'll go to Delphi on the mainland and consult my oracle.
King:	Good idea! I look forward to your return. [Perseus exits left] [to the audience] Well that's that. I'll never see him again and that is the way I want it. All this pretense about Princess Hippodameia can stop and I can get serious about the boy's mother, Danaë. With that boy around I never even had a chance.

[curtain]

SCENE 2: Mount Olympus

Athena and Hermes are deep in conversation.

[curtain]

Athena: I'm telling you I overheard the whole thing. Polydectes is deliberately sending Perseus to his destruction. He is thrilled with the opportunity to rid himself of anything that stands in the way of himself and Danaë, and he knows that Perseus stands in the way.

Hermes: Well, let's go over that again. Perseus offers to obtain Medusa's head for Polydectes and Polydectes takes him up on it. What a silly youth! How does he possibly think he can kill one of the Gorgon sisters?

Athena: He is now on his way to his oracle at Delphi.

Hermes:	Athena, why do you care what happens to Medusa? Years ago you got really annoyed at her and you alone are responsible for her appearance. Why that old hag with terrible teeth, pointed face, protruding tongue, and snake hair is enough to frighten anyone to death.
Athena:	You always like to rub salt in the wounds. Yes, I am responsible for her appearance.
Hermes:	Why do you upset yourself about Medusa?
Athena:	I am not worried about Medusa. I am worried about Perseus. He is a decent fellow.
Hermes:	If you are so worried about Perseus, why don't you help him?
Athena:	That is just what I was going to ask you. Will you help him also? Between the two of us we should be able to help him kill Medusa. He must not look at her or he will turn to stone. [pause] I have it! I will give him my shield. If he polishes it to a bright shine he can look in it as if in a mirror. Then he will not gaze directly on Medusa.
Hermes:	Great! I will give him a good sickle, one so sharp it will cut through the scales on her neck, but he will still need winged sandals, a magic wallet in which to carry the severed head, and a helmet of invisibleness. He can get these but not without difficulty. He will have to go to the Stygian nymphs who are in charge of them. You know, I am in need of a bit of diversion. I think I'll go with him.
Athena:	And if necessary I can meet you. Now let us go meet Perseus and help him. He doesn't have to know who we are. We'll be ordinary people for a few days—ordinary people with extraordinary powers.
Hermes:	Good idea. We can meet him in Samos. I will put an idea in his head that after visiting Delphi he should start his trip from Samos. There he will find pictures of the Gorgons. He can study them so he knows exactly which one is Medusa.

[curtain]

Act III. Challenge of the sisters.

SCENE 1. Dismal wooded area.

Narrator:	Hermes and Athena take over the project of guiding Perseus. They became friendly with Perseus, and since he was in a strange area and rather lonely it wasn't hard for them to develop a relationship. Athena gave him her sheild, admonishing

him to polish it well, and Hermes gave him the sickle. Hermes decided to accompany Perseus to see the three Gray Sisters, who shared one eye among them. They would be the only ones who could tell him the whereabouts of their sisters, the Gorgons, and the location of the Stygian nymphs. Hermes convinced Perseus that these two visits were a must.

[curtain]

Enter Enyo, Deino, and Pemphredo.

Enyo: It is my turn to have the eye. Now you give it to me.

Deino: No, it is not. You had our eye for a long time this morning.

Pemphredo: Stop it, both of you. It is my turn and you both know it. Now give me the eye. You two sometimes act disgracefully.

Enyo: Look who is talking, Miss Virtue herself.

Deino: That's right. Who do you think you are? You are no better than we are and you have no right to be preachy to us. You are no older. We are all young old ones. Isn't that funny? Young old ones.

Pemphredo: Stop this instant. You are both talking nonsense. Just because we have gray hair doesn't mean we are old. We are just prematurely gray. That's it. Prematurely gray.

Enyo: Now look who is talking nonsense. Give me that eye. I know you are just trying to divert my attention.

[Perseus and Hermes enter stage right in front of the curtain]

Hermes: See them. Isn't that a sketch? Why, they are fighting with each other.

Perseus: Don't let them see us!

Hermes: [interrupting] Perseus! Get yourself together. Of course they can't see us.

Perseus: You're right. Sorry.

Hermes: When one passes the eye to the other, lean in there and grab it.

Perseus: I'm watching. There she goes. [moving onto stage] I've got it.

Enyo:	Where is the eye? Sister, give me the eye.
Deino:	I gave it to you.
Enyo:	Stop teasing me. It is very frustrating.
Pemphredo:	This bickering must stop now. I swear you are both acting like babies.
Perseus:	Listen to me, fair ladies. I have the eye.
Gray Sisters:	[silence for a few seconds] You have the eye? Who are you?
Perseus:	I am Perseus. I came here from Seriphos to ask you where the Stygian nymphs live. I need to see them.
Gray Sisters:	We don't know what you are talking about. We do not know any nymphs.
Perseus:	Now I think you are teasing me. If you do not tell me where the Stygian nymphs live, you will not get your eye back. You are in no position to bargain. Just tell me where the nymphs live and how to get to them. And tell me where your sisters, the Gorgons, live.
Pemphredo:	I'll take charge here, girls. You are right of course. We do know where the nymphs live and of course we know where our sisters live, but we have very little to do with them. But how do I know that you will give the eye back once we tell you?
Perseus:	You don't of course. But trust me. I will swear by the god Hermes that I will give it back.
Pemphredo:	That is good enough for me. I've always had great respect for Hermes even though he is a rogue. It will not be an easy trip. You must follow the North Wind. Go beyond where the North Wind lives and then on to the Hyperboreans. Just beyond there you will find the nymphs. When you leave there, head due south until you come to an island very close to the River Ocean in the far west. There you will find our sisters, the Gorgons. But take care, it is a long journey.
Perseus:	I'm glad you saw fit to tell me. Now here is your eye back. [gives it to Pemphredo]
Deino:	Who's got the eye? Who's got the eye? This isn't fair.
Enyo:	No, this isn't fair.
Hermes:	[from his position in front of curtain] Come on, Perseus. Let them figure it out themselves.

[curtain]

SCENE 2. Bare trees, howling wind.

Narrator: The trip went well; however, Perseus had a hard time keeping up with Hermes who took such long strides. Hermes sympathized with Perseus and he lent the young man his staff. From then on Perseus had no difficulty keeping up. The Stygian nymphs were gracious and without question produced the winged sandals, magic wallet, and invisible helmet. With just a little instruction, Perseus was able to fly right along with Hermes. It wasn't very long until they arrived at the Gorgon's encampment in a valley surrounded by oak trees and not far from where the River Ocean flowed.

[curtain]

Enter Hermes and Perseus at stage right. [spotlight on them]

Hermes: [pointing] Turn your shield at an angle and look into it. Be careful. You do not want to take a chance. Now make sure that you recognize Medusa. Get the sickle ready.

Perseus: [studying reflection in his shield] I'm ready. I see her. Great. They are all sleeping.

Hermes: Now is your chance.

Narrator: Perseus cuts the head off with one blow and quickly puts it in his magic wallet that expanded to take care of the size. It was a terrible scene. Pegasus, the winged horse, and Chrysaor, a creature of monstrous shape, were immediately born from the blood of Medusa. Perseus almost went into shock with this event, but Hermes encouraged him to leave at once. Since he had on his invisible helmet, Perseus could not be found by the other Gorgon Sisters. As Perseus and Hermes flew home, Hermes helped him carry the heavy head. They hugged the coast of North Africa until they passed the Nile River. They then headed north passing over an area known as Ethiopia. There, Hermes left him, as Perseus wasn't too far from home. Shortly after Hermes's departure Perseus noticed a maiden in distress on a steep precipice. He swooped down to investigate.

Act IV. A monster and a marriage.

SCENE 1. A hillside in Ethiopia.

Andromeda is tied to a stake.

Perseus: What brings this terrible misfortune to you?

[curtain]

Andromeda: You better get away from here before the monster from the sea comes.

Perseus: You didn't answer me. [untying Andromeda] What is the cause of this problem? Who are you?

Andromeda: I am Andromeda, the daughter of King Cepheus and Cassiopeia. My mother irritated the sea nymphs in some way and apparently they demanded revenge.

Perseus: You don't know what your mother did? Come now!

Andromeda: Well, yes I do. She acted in a silly and vain manner and boasted that she was more beautiful than the sea goddesses, so Poseidon sent a serpent to ravage the land. For months he has terrorized the young maidens, grasping and killing them.

Perseus: Buy why would this mean that you would be deliberately chained out here?

Andromeda: My father was told that the only way to stop this wholesale ravage was to sacrifice me. I know they are grieving about this.

Perseus: You are the most beautiful maiden that I have ever seen. Come with me and be my wife. Please don't back off from me. I am not the monster. I am Perseus, grandson of the king of Argolis.

Andromeda: You are a handsome young man, and you seem to gentle and kind—I would gladly be your wife.

King Cepheus: [entering from left] I overheard this conversation. Sir, if you would get rid of the serpent, for the monster is a serpent, you have my permission to wed my daughter and to take her with you to your own country.

Perseus: Then it is settled. I will await the serpent and slay him.

[Perseus, Andromeda, and Cepheus freeze on stage while narrator speaks]

Narrator: Perseus didn't have to wait long. Within a matter of minutes, the hideous serpent was seen climbing swiftly to the hilltop. Perseus met the challenge with a sword and soon the serpent lay dead. Andromeda wept for joy.

Perseus: King Cepheus, the serpent is dead. I claim you daughter and look forward to being your son-in-law.

King Cepheus: Let us take a little time and think about this. You are asking a great deal. The thought of losing my dear daughter almost breaks my heart. And I know that her mother will be stricken. She has been in the palace crying for four days over this unfortunate situation.

Perseus:	Good king, you forgot your promise to me very quickly. I insist that a bargain is a bargain and I want to make Andromeda my wedded wife.
King Cepheus:	I insist that the whole bargain, as you call it, was made too hastily. A bargain made under duress is really no bargain at all.
Andromeda:	Father, I will say something. I wish to be the wife of this courageous young man who has saved me from such awful terrors. I absolutely insist upon it. If you do not give us the proper wedding that is rightfully ours, I will run away with him and you will then truly lose me. I am astonished at your behavior as I have always known you to be an honorable man. You taught me justice. Now where is your justice?
King Cepheus:	I stand corrected. Perseus, I am sorry. I wish you to come to our home and we will make plans for the wedding.

[curtain]

SCENE 2. Palace of King Cepheus.

King Cepheus, Perseus, Andromeda, and Queen Cassiopeia are on stage.

[curtain]

King Cepheus:	Come dear friends and join in a toast to the engaged couple, Andromeda and Perseus.
Cassiopeia:	Yes, a toast to Perseus and Andromeda. [to Perseus] May you appreciate the beauty of our daughter. Her beauty, of course, is not as lovely as mine, but next to me, she is the most beautiful creature alive.
King Cepheus:	Woman! Have you learned nothing from our recent experience? You know that the goddesses are the most beautiful.
Cassiopeia:	Of course, the goddesses are the exceptions. But still, our beauty is something to behold.
King Cepheus:	Cassiopeia, please! Forget this for now.
Phineus:	[entering from left] What is this all about? Andromeda is betrothed to me. You know this. What is this treachery? My dear Andromeda, what is happening?
King Cepheus:	I will answer for you, daughter. Phineus, where were you when Andromeda needed you? I didn't hear you say anything about your betrothal? No, you weren't willing to speak up about it then. By your absence on that hillside, you broke your betrothal. It was obvious to all. Andromeda found a real man.

Phineus:	Those are poorly chosen words, sir.
Perseus:	You are outnumbered. Accept this and give no trouble.
Phineus:	For the moment perhaps. [exits left]
Perseus:	Soon to be father-in-law, in order for Andromeda to adjust to married life and to ease her departure, I will stay here for a year. This will enable us to get acquainted and it will be beneficial to all.
Andromeda:	Thank you, dear Perseus.

[curtain]

Narrator:	It wasn't long before Phineus was back, this time with an entourage of about two hundred men. Since he wouldn't listen to reason, Perseus pulled out Medusa's head and turned the whole group into stone. The months passed by serenely and Andromeda gave birth to a beautiful baby boy, whom the parents named Perse. Shortly after the birth of Perse, the young couple left for Seriphos, leaving little Perse behind to be brought up by his grandparents.

SCENE 3. The palace of Polydectes in Seriphos.

Polydectes and three friends are present.

Polydectes:	[noise outside] What is the noise and confusion outside?
Adviser:	I'll go and see what it is all about.
Polydectes:	[to the guests] Enjoy yourselves. This is a great party. Bring more delectables. [aside to another aide] What is all that noise?
Perseus:	[entering left] So this is where I find you? And my dear mother? I understand that you have tormented her because she would not have you for a husband. What kind of man are you? She tells me that no sooner was I gone when you pestered her unmercifully. Finally, as a last resort my mother and Dictys had to take refuge in a temple where you would not dare to touch her. I've been to that temple, sir. I have talked to that lovely lady who is my mother. [Polydectes backs off] Yes, back up. Think of your sins. Think of your treachery. You will have plenty of time. By the way, here is your present.
Narrator:	As you suspected, Perseus took the head of Medusa out of his magic wallet and showed it to Polydectes and the assembled guests. The stones are probably still standing there. Perseus took Andromeda and Danaë to Argolis leaving Dictys on the throne of Seriphos. Perseus accidentally, or so it seems, struck Danaë's father with a discus and he died instantly. Perseus and Andromeda lived happily ever after.

[curtain]

TEACHERS' NOTES

1. Using transparency number 1, ask the students what part of the world they see. Write on the transparency: Southern Europe, Near East, North Africa, and the Mediterranean Sea. Give students a blank map and have them lightly color all water with blue pencil. Using transparency number 5, ask them to locate the following places on their maps: Hyperboreans, Stygian nymphs, Gorgons, Mount Atlas, the Gray Sisters, Cimmerians, Delphi, Argolis, Tiryns, Seriphos, Samos, and Joppa. Explain to the students that in this play Ethiopia is believed to be an area around Joppa.

2. The adventures of Perseus were very popular and recounted many times in ancient Greece; however, there are many versions. Robert Graves tells us that Perseus, although found by Dictys was actually reared by King Polydectes.[1] On the other hand, Edith Hamiltion tells us that Perseus was reared by Dictys and his wife.[2] There is variance as to where the nymphs and where the Gorgons lived. In addition the Gray Sisters (sometimes referred to as the Graeae) reportedly lived at the foot of Mount Atlas, in North Africa, behind the Cimmerians, and behind the Hyperboreans.

3. Some accounts have Perseus not giving the eye back. He keeps it and then drops it in the sea.

Perseus **Transparency Master no. 5.**

VOCABULARY

admonish. to warn a person to behave in a specific manner

betrothal. engagement to be married

devastate. to ruin or destroy completely

diversion. to turn aside, distract

duress. the use of force or threats to make someone do something

invisibleness. unable to be seen

premature. too early or too hasty; before the correct time

pretense. a false claim, excuse or show

protrude. to stick out, extend

sickle. a tool with a curved blade and short handle

ACTIVITIES

1. Make a map of Perseus's adventures.

2. Illustrate the adventures of Perseus in a comic strip much like Prince Valiant.

3. Make flash cards for all the characters in Perseus. Have one student try to go through the cards without making a mistake. When a mistake is made, start over with a new student. As an alternative, students could sit in pairs, make the flash cards, and then quiz one another.

4. Have an art contest with students drawing Medusa. Give a prize for the ugliest.

5. Save the classified sections of the newspapers. Give each student a page of classified ads. On this page the student should draw a character from the play, either doing a close up showing only the head or the whole body in action. Color with crayons rubbing in well. Then select one color of water-based poster paint and brush over the colored picture. Let dry. This is very effective artwork to display in the room.

DISCUSSION QUESTIONS

Name_____

Perseus Act I

1. What relation is Dictys to the king?

2. Even on the beach under extraordinary circumstances, how does Dictys abide by the rules of hospitality?

3. How do you know that Dictys does not have a warm relationship with the king?

4. How might Perseus's life have been different had his grandfather not consulted an oracle?

5. How would Perseus's childhood and youth have been the same regardless of where he was brought up?

6. Do you think Danaë made the right decision to live with Dictys?

7. What would have been different about Danaë's life had she lived with Polydectes?

8. Research the Hyperboreans, Gray Sisters, (sometimes called the Graeae), and the Gorgons.

Name_____

Perseus Act II

1. Whom does Polydectes say that he is going to marry?

2. Do you believe Polydectes? Why or why not?

3. What does Hermes think of Perseus when he hears that the youth is about to go after Medusa?

4. What are the three things that Hermes says Perseus must get from the Stygian nymphs?

5. Why was it rather easy for Hermes and Athena to establish a relationship with Perseus?

6. What might have happened to Perseus had he not had the help of the gods?

7. How do you explain Perseus's decision to bring home the head of Medusa?

8. Research why Athena turned Medusa into such an ugly being.

Name_____

Perseus Act III

1. Where did the Gray Sisters live?

2. What caused a conflict between the sisters?

3. Which sister seemed to be in charge?

4. How do you feel about Perseus taking advantage of someone's handicap? How do people today sometimes take advantage of the handicapped?

5. What would have happened to Perseus had he not looked into the shield but instead looked directly at Medusa?

6. Do you think there was another way to kill Medusa?

7. What kept Medusa's sisters from following Perseus?

8. Compare Theseus and Perseus. The topic sentence might be: "Many aspects of Theseus and Perseus's lives were similar."

Name_____

Perseus **Act IV**

1. Why is Andromeda tied on the mountainside?

2. What prompted Cepheus to offer his daughter to Perseus?

3. Why was Perseus so taken with Andromeda?

4. What do you think of Cepheus's attempt to deny his bargain with Perseus? Have you ever had someone go back on a bargain? How did you handle it?

5. Was Cepheus correct in telling Phineus that Phineus had broken the betrothal? Why or why not?

6. What do you think of Perseus and Andromeda's decision to leave their son with the grandparents?

7. What did Perseus and Perse have in common as infants and children?

8. Write a paragraph about Perseus in which you put the events in chronological order. Your topic sentence could be: "Beginning with his decision to kill Medusa, Perseus had a very busy schedule."

TESTS

Name_____

Perseus Test Yourself

Choose the correct word from the list below and fill in the blanks.

Gray Sisters	Seriphos	Pegasus	Hermes
Cassiopeia	shield	Phineus	Cepheus
Cimmerians	Medusa	Danaë	oracle
Hyperboreans	Stygian	Polydectes	Zeus
invisible cap	Acrisius	Hippodameia	Delphi

1. _____The place where Perseus consulted oracle.

2. _____Athena lent Perseus this.

3. _____They had one eye among them.

4. _____She had snake hair.

5. _____Polydectes announced his engagement to her.

6. _____He gave Perseus a sickle.

7. _____These nymphs held items needed by Perseus.

8. _____He brought up Perseus.

9. _____The mother of Perseus.

10. _____Where Greeks went to consult the gods.

11. _____Father of Danaë.

12. _____Polydectes was king here.

13. _____Head god.

14. _____He was born with wings from Medusa's blood.

15. _____She offended the sea nymphs.

16. _____Father of Perseus's bride.

17. _____ Former suitor who demanded Andromeda honor their betrothal.

18. _____ The Stygian nymphs lived north of here.

19. _____ The Gray Sisters lived north of here.

20. _____ Wearing this allowed Perseus to be unseen.

Name_____

Perseus **Final Test**

Choose the correct answer and write the corresponding number in the parentheses.

( )   1. The Gray Sisters seemed to: (a) get along well (b) bicker with each other (c) not speak at all.

( )   2. Perseus told Polydectes that as an engagement present he would bring home: (a) Medusa's head (b) a Stygian nymph (c) a winged horse.

( )   3. Perseus: (a) gave the stolen eye back (b) dropped the eye in the sea (c) gave the eye to Polydectes.

( )   4. Athena cautioned Perseus: (a) to keep a good one hundred feet away from Medusa (b) to throw cold water at Medusa (c) to polish the shield to a good shine.

( )   5. Hermes taught Perseus to fly with: (a) wings on his shoulders (b) wings on his sandals (c) wings on his hat.

( )   6. The goddess responsible for Medusa's frightening looks was: (a) Hera (b) Iris (c) Athena.

( )   7. Polydectes hoped that Perseus would: (a) die in the attempt to kill Medusa (b) become a hero (c) bring honor upon the island.

( )   8. Athena enlisted the help of: (a) Hera (b) Zeus (c) Hermes.

( )   9. Athena said: (a) "We'll be ordinary people for a few days" (b) "We'll tell Perseus we are gods" (c) "We'll get Zeus to tell him we are gods."

( )   10. At Samos, Perseus saw pictures of: (a) the Gray Sisters (b) the nymphs (c) the Gorgons.

( )   11. Pemphredo said she always had great respect for: (a) Hermes (b) Hera (c) Athena.

( )   12. Cepheus wanted to: (a) kill the serpent threatening his daughter (b) renege on his promise to Perseus (c) postpone the wedding until the following year.

( )   13. Pegasus, the winged horse, was born from the blood of: (a) Medusa (b) the Stygian nymphs (c) the serpent who was looking for Andromeda.

( )   14. Perseus put the Medusa's severed head in: (a) a backpack (b) a purse (c) a magic wallet.

( )   15. The woman who irritated the sea nymphs was: (a) Danaë (b) Cassiopeia (c) Athena.

( )   16. Cepheus said his bargain with Perseus was made: (a) when he was hypnotized (b) when he was under duress (c) when he was ill.

( )   17. Cepheus accused Andromeda's former fiance of: (a) deserting her when she was in need (b) looking out for himself (c) seeking glory.

( )   18. Perseus and Andromeda left their baby boy with: (a) Athena (b) Polydectes (c) Cepheus.

( )   19. The Gray Sisters lived in a land: (a) bright and cheerful (b) dark and gray (c) neither of these.

( )   20. Dictys was: (a) kind and good (b) mean-spirited (c) forgetful.

MYTHO GAME
(*Great Athenian* and *Perseus* combined)

See instructions in the chapter on general activities, page 228.

1. Who was the mother of Theseus?

2. Who was the architect of the labyrinth?

3. Name the friend of Theseus who tried to steal his cattle.

4. What queen of the Amazons did Theseus marry?

5. Name the second wife of Theseus.

6. Who was Theseus's father?

7. Where was Theseus born?

8. Who was the father of Ariadne?

9. Name the son of Medea.

10. How old was Theseus when he moved the boulder?

11. What had Theseus's father put under the boulder?

12. What gulf separates Troezen and Athens?

13. What relation was Theseus to Hercules?

14. Who was king of Athens?

15. How many sons did King Aegeus's half-brother have?

16. With what did Medea try to kill Theseus?

17. Why did King Minos demand tribute from the Athenians?

18. What was the name of the half man and half bull?

19. What was the labyrinth?

20. On what island was the labyrinth?

21. If Theseus returned from the labyrinth safely, what color flag was he to fly?

22. Name a type of government that is the opposite of a democratic government.

23. What did Ariadne give Theseus to help him get out of the labyrinth?

24. Who told Ariadne how Theseus could get out of the labyrinth?

25. On what island was Ariadne left?

26. Who were the sisters with one eye?

27. Name the father of Danaë.

28. Who reared Perseus?

29. What kind of hair did Medusa have?

30. Who found Danaë?

31. What god gave Perseus a sickle?

32. What goddess lent Perseus a shield?

33. Who kept the cap of invisibleness?

34. The Gray Sisters lived far north of what people?

35. The Stygian nymphs lived far beyond what people?

36. What was the name of the river that flows around the known earth in both directions?

37. What in Andromeda's mother's character offended the sea goddesses?

38. Who was Andromeda's father?

39. How long did Perseus and Andromeda live with her parents after marriage?

40. What did Perseus show Polydectes that killed the latter?

41. With what did Perseus accidentally hit his grandfather and kill him?

42. What was Ariadne's sister's name?

43. What was the name of Antiope and Theseus's son?

44. What happens to the person who dies and does not receive proper burial?

45. What is the name today of the Euxine Sea?

46. In a marriage to an Amazon woman, who did the proposing?

47. Who was the god of war?

48. Who won the war between the Athenians and the Amazons?

49. How was Antiope killed?

50. Who rescued Theseus from the Underworld?

PERSEUS **CROSSWORD PUZZLE CLUES**

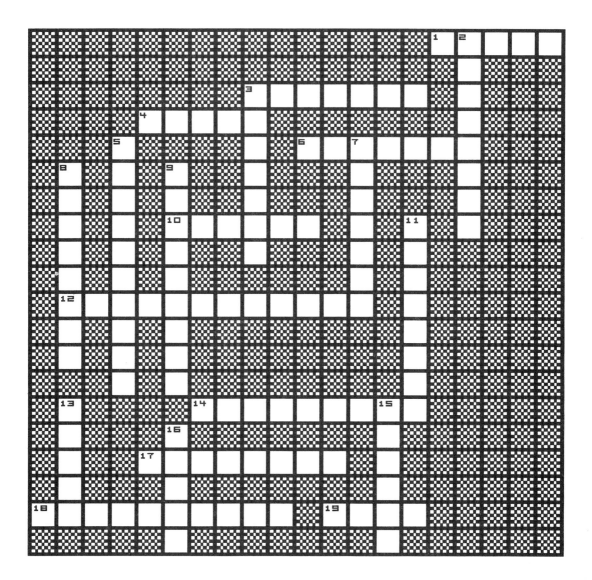

Across

1. Athena and Hermes met Perseus here
3. Winged horse
4. Name of Perseus' son
6. He tried to break his bargain
10. She has snakes for hair
12. The nymphs lived just beyond these people
14. Daughter of King Cepheus
17. Born from the blood of Medusa
18. King of Seriphos
19. One of the Gray Sisters

Down

2. King of Argolis
3. Son of Danaë
5. Her problem was vanity
7. Suitor of Andromeda
8. Dictys lived here
9. One of the Gray Sisters
11. Andromeda was tied to a stake here
13. One of the Gray Sisters
15. A fisherman
16. The number of things the Stygian nymphs gave Perseus

NOTES

1. Robert Graves, *The Greek Myths*, (New York: Viking-Penguin, 1960), 1:238.

2. Edith Hamilton, *Mythology*, (New York: New American Library, 1940), 143.

Persephone

THE PLAY

Cast of Characters
In Order of Appearance

Narrator
Nymph #1, playmate of Persephone
Persephone, daughter of Demeter
Nymph #2, playmate of Persephone
Hades, god of the Underworld
Demeter, goddess of grain
Hecate, goddess of the dark of the moon
Helios, sun god
Princess, daughter of Metaneira
Metaneira, wife of King Celeus
Zeus, king of gods
Hermes, messenger of Zeus

SCENE 1. A meadow of flowers at the seashore's edge.

Persephone and three sea nymphs are picking flowers.

Narrator: Demeter, the goddess of grain, who spent most of her time on earth attending to her duties with the crops, was the mother of a lovely young daughter. They lived on the island of Sicily far away from the other gods and goddesses. Occasionally she left Persephone for a few hours while she looked out for her interests. Persephone behaved nicely while her mother was away and this particular day was no different; she had her mother's permission to go down to the shore and play with the sea nymphs.

[curtain]

Nymph #1:   Come, Persephone, come here and see these beautiful flowers. They are truly lovely.

Persephone: Just a minute, sweet friend. I am gathering some narcissus, surely the fairest of them all. [she leans to pick one at the edge of the bluff]

Nymph #2:   Do be careful, Persephone. Your mother, Demeter, would never forgive us if anything happened to you. You are her joy, the light of her life.

Persephone: I know that, dear friend, and so I will never take chances. I am safe. But let me see your flowers. Yes, you are right. They are exquisite flowers.

Nymph #1:   Oh! Look at the beautiful ferns. Come here Persephone.

Nymph #2:   [leaning over ferns at stage left] See how tall they are. I guess it is because they are sometimes in the sun.

Nymph #1: Speaking of the sun reminds me that we must not get parched; we cannot stay much longer. We need to get wet. Remember, Mother told us not to stay in the sun too long. Where is Persephone?

Persephone: [a great rumbling is heard as she pulls up a root and nymphs scurry for cover] What noise do I hear? [Hades comes up through the hole made when root was pulled up] Who are you? What manner of man are you to come up through the earth? [looking around] Where are my friends? [nymph peeks out from edge of rock]

Hades: My little sweetheart, do not be afraid. I wish to make you queen of the Underworld. You will have gold jewelry set with gorgeous diamonds. You will have everything and anything you desire. You will really like it there. The palace is magnificent. Imagine being a queen!

Persephone: I don't want to be a queen. Leave me alone. [Hades moves closer to her] Don't you dare touch me.

Hades: [snatching Persephone by the hand] Come with me, my little one. Come and ride in my gold chariot.

Persephone: Mother, dear Mother. Please help me. I need you. Mother! Mother!

Hades: Come. Don't fight me little one. You will be happy in your new home, I promise you. There will be all sorts of things for you to play with. I need you there. I feel lonely sometimes with only the souls of the dead for company. [He drags Persephone to the open hole]

Persephone: Mother! Mother! [thunderous music; Persephone and Hades do not exit either left or right; rather they disappear straight down; the earth has opened up and swallowed them]

[enter Demeter; one sea nymph peeking from behind boulder]

Demeter: I know my precious daughter is somewhere near. [sees nymph peeking out from behind rock] Tell me, have you seen my lovely daughter, Persephone?

Nymph #1: I cannot say. Only trouble will be mine if I tell you what I saw.

Demeter: Come little one. Do not be afraid. Tell me exactly what you saw.

Nymph #1: I cannot say. I didn't see anyone except a young girl who was picking narcissus. My sister and I were playing with her. She strayed a short distance from us. The last I saw her she was kneeling by those flowers over there. [points to spot where Persephone disappeared]

Demeter:	Was this girl Persephone?
Nymph #1:	(faintly) Yes, it was Persephone.
Persephone:	[from offstage] Mother! Mother!
Demeter:	Yes, Persephone. Here I am. Do you hear me? Where are you? Persephone. Persephone. Can you hear me? [Persephone calls again] I hear her calling me. Truly, she must be nearby, but she doesn't answer me. [Demeter sits in front of curtain at stage right] I will make a journey to see Hecate. That miserable woman knows everything.

[curtain]

SCENE 2. Dark cave.

Hecate leaning on broom, faces the audience.

[curtain]

Hecate:	I live alone here. It is dark, cold and miserable all of which helps me feel good. However, I am so busy haunting the crossroads at midnight, taking care of the hounds that always follow me, and keeping tabs on evildoers that I scarcely have time to enjoy being miserable.
Demeter:	[enters from left] Hello, miserable woman. How are you today?
Hecate:	Wretched, as usual, which makes me very happy.
Demeter:	That certainly sounds dismal.
Hecate:	I just love to be miserable. I am the happiest when I am unhappy and lonely. I hate everything and everybody. Oh, how happy I am.
Demeter:	I know you never miss anything. Have you seen my daughter, Persephone? She disappeared while picking flowers.
Hecate:	And what reason is that to bother a cantankerous old woman? Tell me something really bad so I can feel joyful.
Demeter:	For me, Persephone being gone is as bad as things can get. Please tell me what you know.

Hecate: What I know? What I know? I don't like to tell all I know.

Demeter: Please, Hecate! Tell me some bad news. You certainly know all the bad news around, so help make me sadder than I already am and we can be miserable together.

Hecate: You're bothering me. Go visit Helios. Now there is a god that knows everything. I'd go with you but I can't stand the bright lights. Now be gone and leave me to be forlorn. I love it.

Demeter: You're right. Helios sees everything in his travels. I will go and ask Helios. [she again sits in front of curtain at stage right]

[curtain]

SCENE 3. Western end of the earth at dusk.

Enter Helios who then sits on bench.

Helios: What a hard day! I love a day when my light shines upon the earth. Today my light was interrupted in most parts by the clouds that Zeus, the Cloudgatherer, put in my way. It was no fun racing my chariot through them. I must speak to Zeus about it someday. But who is this? [enter Demeter] Why Demeter, what brings you here?

Demeter: Please tell me. Have you, in the course of your long day, seen my daughter, Persephone? She is such a young girl. I hear her crying for me but I cannot find her.

Helios: Yes, sit here while I tell you what I know. [he pats the bench]

Demeter: [sits down] Be quick, tell me. My heart is broken.

Helios: What I have to tell you will not mend it.

Demeter: Be quick, tell me. I can't stand the delay.

Helios: Hades came from the Underworld and took her with him in his chariot. When she is older he intends to make her his bride. [Demeter gasps] He spotted her as she was picking flowers and from then on there was no changing his mind. I have seen her. She refuses to eat and wants only to return to you. But Hades is a powerful god and I have no influence over him. He is content with darkness and doesn't pay any attention to me.

Demeter: I will think of a way.

[curtain]

SCENE 4: Palace of King Celeus at Eleusis.

Sitting on bench in front of open curtain downstage right, Demeter, dressed in the clothes of a poor peasant, seems lost in thought. Lights on stage are dimmed, spotlight on Demeter.

[curtain]

Demeter: [to audience] I have it. Until my daughter is home again, nothing will grow on this earth. There will be a drought. The wheat, corn, barley, rice, even the fruits and vegetables will wither and die. Nothing will grow while the goddess of grain suffers so. When my child is returned to me, I'll give attention to earthly matters, and not until then.

[enter two young princesses, one of whom speaks to Demeter; lights remain dim on stage while spotlight is on characters]

Princess: You seem very sad. Why are you sitting here all alone?

Demeter: I have nowhere to go; I have no home. I am destitute so I just sit and grieve for the past. Yes, just grieve for the past.

Princess: Could we help you?

Demeter: [looking up] I have a daughter just about your age. She, too, is beautiful. I miss her so much.

Princess: If you like children so much why don't you come home with me and meet my mother. Do you know about babies? Do you know how to take care of them?

Demeter: Unless things have changed a great deal in the last few years, I certainly know how to handle babies.

Princess: Then come home with us. We know our mother, the queen, will be glad to have you in order to have help with our baby brother. He has been sick and he takes all our mother's time. She really is at her wits' end.

Demeter: You are very thoughtful to speak to an old woman like myself and thoughtful too, to be concerned about your mother and baby brother. I will accompany you to your home. Perhaps your mother does need me.

[spotlight goes off and lights brighten on stage; Queen Metaneira, holding a baby, is rocking in a chair, singing a lullaby; enter Demeter and two princesses from in front of curtain]

Metaneira: Come in, come in. My dear girls, who do you bring with you?

Princess: Mother, this is a woman whom we just met. She is lonely and has no relatives nearby. She has nowhere to go; she has no home.

Metaneira: For goodness sake, how did you come to such a pass? Let me offer you a glass of wine.

Demeter: Do not trouble yourself. I prefer plain water with perhaps a bit of barley in it. But please don't fuss for me. You asked me how I came to such a pass. It is hard to believe, but I was kidnapped by pirates and then abandoned on your shores.

Metaneira: Glory! What a devastating situation.

Demeter: [taking the baby in her arms] What a sweet child, but he is thin and peaked. [she holds him close to her] What is his name?

Metaneira: Demophoön.

Demeter: What a lovely name. Little fellow, what makes you fret so?

[Metaneira rises from rocking chair and Demeter sits down and quietly rocks baby, who almost instantly becomes quiet]

Metaneira: He has been so fussy lately. Even the king wonders what is wrong with him. His sisters never gave this kind of trouble. But what am I saying? Look at how peacefully he rests in your arms! And he is not asleep, just quiet as though he were a little god.

Demeter: Yes, he did quiet down, didn't he. What a little love.

Metaneira: You have such a way with a baby. I would truly appreciate it if you would give some thought to remaining with us. We would treat you well.

Demeter: You have already been most gracious. Since I enjoy the duties of motherhood and since this baby seems to be happy in my arms, I will stay.

Metaneira: You will not regret your decision. Come girls. Help me for a moment. I must give the maids word about fixing a room for our new lady and I want one of you to take a message to your father. He is in the throne room at this hour. [girls follow mother off left]

Demeter: I will give you eternal youth in gratitude for all the kindness your mother and sisters are showing me. In order to do this I must place you on the fire every evening. So sleep little baby and do not be afraid of the flames. I am a goddess and I will protect you from injury. [walks over to fireplace and bends over the flames]

Metaneira: [enters from left] What are you doing? Why are you trying to burn my son, you ungrateful creature.

Demeter: [now in glowing robes, see production notes in the general activities chapter] I am Demeter, goddess of the grain. I am the earth goddess. I was giving your son eternal youth, but now you have insulted me. In order to reconcile yourself with the gods, you must build a temple here in my honor. I must leave. [exits left]

Metaneira: I have offended a goddess. Our lives are ruined. [she sits weeping as lights dim]

[curtain]

SCENE 5. Mount Olympus.

Enter Zeus and Hermes in earnest conversation.

[curtain]

Zeus: I have to take a stand with Demeter. That is why I've sent for you, Hermes. The poor mortals on earth are starving because the crops are drying up and dying. Demeter will have to come to her senses.

Hermes: She will not restore the earth until she has her daughter back. She has turned her back on each Olympian you have sent to plead with her.

Zeus: I suppose I'll have to get out my thunderbolts and really stir up a storm ...

Hermes: [interrupting] Father, even that will not change her, or bring her around as you say.

Zeus: Very well. She is carrying this grief business too far. I can see I need to speak to Hades.

Hermes: That's it. Go around Demeter. She is not listening to anyone, even you. So you might just as well go directly to Hades.

Zeus: Go immediately to the Underworld and tell Hades that it is my will that Persephone be allowed to return to her mother. However, the Fates have decreed that she should not return if she has eaten. I am told that she has not eaten since arriving and if this is truly the case she should be returned immediately.

Hermes: It is my understanding that she nibbled on a pomegranate seed.

Zeus: Then definitely some compromise is in order. But go now and bring Persephone back to her mother. Tell Hades that we will do as the Fates decide. Persephone will stay part of the year with him and part with her mother. In that way the mortals on earth will have spring and they will have crops. Have you got that straight?

Hermes: When have I relayed an incorrect message from the gods? [he exits right]

Zeus: That young man always has to have the last word. Someday he will learn that it isn't necessary. But I won't worry about it, because he is dependable and certainly swift.

[curtain]

SCENE 6. Dried and withered field.

[curtain]

Enter Demeter, who walks slowly to front of stage to address audience.

Demeter:	What a pity! The earth is barren. The trees, vines, and crops that were once so luxuriant are now withered and dried. I know that Hades has my dear daughter. Zeus must have known about the abduction and did nothing to stop it. I cannot forgive him for this treachery. My heart is broken.
Persephone:	[from offstage left] Mother! Mother!
Demeter:	[turning toward sound of voice] My own sweet daughter! I hear your voice. Where are you?
Persephone:	[voice closer] I am coming, Mother.
Demeter:	[Persephone enters from left] My own Persephone! [clasping Persephone in her arms] My own daughter!
Persephone:	Mother, I missed you so. My heart was so sad and so dreary. I still can't figure why Hades took me, or for that matter why I am back here again! Hermes came for me and brought me to the nearby woods but he asked me a strange question. He wanted to know if I had eaten any pomegranate seeds? Now isn't that a silly question?
Demeter:	Actually, it is an important question. Did you?
Persephone:	[looking frightened] Yes, I did eat one. Does it really matter?
Demeter:	[gasping] My sweet child, it is a disaster for us. It means that you will have to spend a portion of each year in the Underworld with Hades. While you are gone, I will see to it that nothing will grow. It will be winter and I will be in mourning. But I will look forward to the coming of spring.

[curtain]

TEACHERS' NOTES

1. Using transparency number 1, ask the students what part of the world they see. Write on the transparency: Southern Europe, Near East, North Africa, and the Mediterranean Sea. Give students a blank map and have them lightly color all water with blue pencil. Using transparency number 6, ask them to locate the following places on their maps: Hyperboreans, Hecate's dwelling, Helios' abode, Sicily, Mount Olympus, and Eleusis.

2. Just where Hades kidnapped Persephone is unknown. It could have been Sicily, Crete, Arcadia, or any number of places. The author chose Sicily.

3. The Underworld is an interesting place. The new ghosts are judged daily by Minos, Rhadamanthus, and Aeacus. Minos and Rhadamanthus are brothers. Robert Graves, in his book *The Greek Myths*, divides the Underworld into three parts: the Asphodel Meadows, Tartarus, and the Elysian Fields. The meadows, according to Graves, were for those who were neither virtuous nor evil; Tartarus was for those who were definitely evil; and the Elysian Fields were for the virtuous.[1]

4. The River Styx is used when taking a solemn oath. There seems to be a difference of opinion as to its exact location. According to Graves, Charon ferries newly dead across the Styx to reach the gates of the Underworld. "When ghosts descend to Tartarus, the main entrance to which lies in a grove of black poplars beside the ocean stream, each is supplied by pious relatives with a coin laid under the tongue of its corpse. They are thus able to pay Charon, the miser who ferries them in a crazy boat across the Styx."[2] Hamilton says that Virgil is the only poet who clearly gives the geography of the Underworld and he writes "the path down to it leads to where the Acheron, the river of woe, pours into Cocytus, the river of lamentation. An aged boatman named Charon ferries the souls of the dead across the waters to the farther bank."[3]

5. The bodies of the dead must have proper burial as is noted in the case of Elpenor in *The Odyssey* and in the case of the Thebans in *The Greatest Athenian*. If they do not have proper burial their souls wander aimlessly.

6. Cerberus is a monster dog who guards the entrance to the Underworld. Some say that he has fifty heads, some say he has three. Cerberus allows no one to pass unless they throw him a piece of bread. According to Isaac Asimov, Cerberus did not allow anyone "to pass who did not first throw him a ransom in the form of a piece of bread. For that reason, the phrase 'to throw a sop to Cerberus' means to pay a bribe to some official in order to get something done."[4]

7. Hades is a terrible god and one to fear, but he is not portrayed as evil in mythology. He actually has no home nor does his kingdom have a name, at least in earlier works. Hades comes from a Greek word meaning the unseen and his home is the house of the unseen or Hades.[5]

**The Plight of Persephone and Psyche
Transparency Master no. 6**

VOCABULARY

cantankerous. ready to quarrel

compromise. each party gives up part of what he wants

destitute. not having, being without, lacking

dismal. causing gloom or misery

drought. long period with little or no rain

eternal. lasting forever

exquisite. very beautiful

mourn. to be sad or show sorrow over a loss

oblivious. not noticing, not mindful

parch. to become dry and hot

scurry. run quickly, scamper

wither. to dry up

witness. a person who saw, or can give, a firsthand account of something that happened

ACTIVITIES

1. Have students draw their own maps of the Underworld. There is no right or wrong way to do this. Let them use their imaginations. Have them mark the entrance. Is it outside River Ocean as it was in the *Odyssey*, or is it near some far distant lonely place such as north of where the Cimmerians live or down south near Taenarus?

2. Make an imaginary game called "The Underworld." Tokens could be various heroes. The students could work in groups, designing their own boards. Each board should have the heroes passing by Cerberus, going over certain rivers, taking a ferry, and drinking blood. Perhaps the idea could be how to survive in Hades.

DISCUSSION QUESTIONS

Name_____

1. In the first scene with whom is Persephone playing?

2. Why do you think the sea nymph was scared to say what she witnessed?

3. What advice does Hecate give Demeter?

4. Some mythologists say that Hecate was an old crone and others say that she was a monster. If you were casting her in a play how would you portray her? Why?

5. What kind of a day does the sun god dislike?

6. Do you think Persephone and her mother were close? Why or why not?

7. How would you have handled the problem if you were Zeus?

8. Research Hecate.

TESTS

Name_____

Persephone **Test Yourself**

Choose the correct word from the list below and fill in the blanks. Each word is used once.

Hermes	Hades	Zeus
Hecate	Demeter	Metaneira
Persephone	Celeus	Helios
nymphs		

1. _____Beautiful young daughter of Demeter.

2. _____King of the gods.

3. _____Messenger of Zeus.

4. _____Goddess of the dark side of moon.

5. _____Ordered to build a temple at Eleusis.

6. _____Father of baby Demophoön.

7. _____God of Underworld.

8. _____Goddess of earth or grain.

9. _____Told Demeter who was holding Persephone.

10. _____Picking flowers with Persephone.

Name_____

Persephone **Final Test**

Choose the correct answer and write the corresponding letter in the parentheses.

(   )   1.   When Demeter found Persephone to be missing she: (a) went to Zeus immediately (b) took to her bed in sorrow (c) searched relentlessly for her.

(   )   2.   Persephone was picking a narcissus when: (a) the earth opened up (b) she fell into the hole (c) she lost her footing.

(   )   3.   Persephone was kidnapped by: (a) Hades (b) Celeus (c) Hermes.

(   )   4.   Hecate advised Demeter to: (a) confer with Zeus (b) build a temple at Eleusis (c) seek out the sun god.

(   )   5.   The sun god: (a) wouldn't say a word (b) said he was too busy racing his chariot to have time to talk to Demeter (c) told her the truth.

(   )   6.   Zeus sent one of the following to visit Hades: (a) Hermes (b) Celeus (c) Iris.

(   )   7.   Persephone: (a) refused to eat the meals prepared for her (b) ate one pomegranate seed (c) drank only water.

(   )   8.   Zeus sent word to Hades that he must: (a) do as Fates decided (b) release Persephone (c) keep Persephone tightly locked up.

(   )   9.   When Demeter arrived at Metaneira's home she was offered: (a) barley water (b) milk (c) wine.

(   ) 10.   Zeus lives: (a) on Mount Olympus (b) most of the time in Athens (c) at the foot of Mount Olympus.

(   ) 11.   Persephone was last seen by: (a) swamp nymphs (b) sea nymphs (c) meadow nymphs.

(   ) 12.   When Hades appeared, the nymphs: (a) scurried for cover (b) boldly faced him (c) jumped back in the water.

(   ) 13.   Hades promised Persephone: (a) all the pomegranates she could eat (b) a ride in his underworld chariot (c) gold jewelry set with gorgeous diamonds.

(   ) 14.   Hecate is only happy when: (a) she is miserable (b) the moon is up (c) things are going right for her.

(   ) 15.   The sun god hates days that are too: (a) bright (b) rainy (c) cloudy.

(   ) 16.   The sun god said he has no influence over: (a) Hades (b) Poseidon (c) Hermes.

(   ) 17.   When Demeter meets her, Metaneira is: (a) doing the laundry (b) singing a lullaby (c) talking to the king.

(   ) 18.   Zeus said that in order to get Persephone back, there would have to be: (a) arbitration (b) mediation (c) compromise.

(   ) 19.   When Demeter arrived at the home, Metaneira's son: (a) was very good (b) had colic (c) was fussy.

(   ) 20.   What happens to Persephone will be decided by: (a) the Fates (b) the Furies (c) the Muses.

NOTES

1. Robert Graves, *The Greek Myths* (New York: Viking-Penguin, 1960), 1:121.

2. Ibid., 1:120.

3. Edith Hamilton, *Mythology* (New York: New American Library, 1940), 39.

4. Isaac Asimov, *Words from the Myths* (Boston: Houghton-Mifflin, 1969), 39.

5. H. J. Rose, *A Handbook of Mythology* (New York: Dutton, 1959), 78.

Psyche

THE PLAY

Cast of Characters
In Order of Appearance

Narrator
King of Miletus, father of Psyche
Queen, mother of Psyche
Zeus, king of gods
Hermes, Zeus's messenger
Aphrodite, goddess of love
Eros, son of Aphrodite
Psyche, daughter of King Miletus
Zephyr, West Wind
Voice, Eros in disguise
Sister #1, sister of Psyche
Sister #2, sister of Psyche
Demeter, goddess of grain
Hera, queen of gods
Custom, Aphrodite's caretaker
Anxiety and Sorrow, two grim women
Voice of the tower
Ghost, servant in Underworld
Persephone, queen of the Underworld

Act I. The beginning.

SCENE 1. King's palace.

[curtain]

King: [to his wife] Our two older daughters have made good marriages. I fully expected that our third daughter, Psyche, would have made a handsome match by this time. Instead no one calls at all.

Queen: That is not true. Princes come from afar to see her ...

King: [interrupting] Yes, they come from afar to see her. Yes, to see her, but not to court her. Not one has asked for her hand in marriage. Not one has come to the palace.

Queen: When she goes into the town, people stop and gaze at her. She can't have any kind of a normal life. All people stare at her and now they are even worshipping her like she was a goddess.

King: I've heard of this. How true is it? If folks are really worshipping her, like it is said, there will be big trouble from Aphrodite, the goddess of beauty. We are in for trouble.

Queen: I cannot think our darling Psyche would deliberately bring trouble upon us. She is the sweetest of all three of our daughters. She is certainly the most beautiful. And yes it is true that some folks are worshiping her. I understand that this is adversely affecting the worship at Aphrodite's temple.

King: This is bad news. Call the servants. I want my things packed as I must go visit my oracle Apollo. There I will get the help I need.

Queen: Dear husband, take me with you. I want to hear what the oracle has to say with my own ears.

[curtain]

SCENE 2. Mount Olympus, the garden.

Zeus and Hermes are seated on a bench.

[curtain]

Zeus: I can't believe this. That mere child Psyche is being treated like she was a goddess. Did you say that Aphrodite's temples are being deserted?

Hermes: This is true, Father. The people have decided that Psyche is really none other than Aphrodite who has decided to live on earth rather than Olympus.

Zeus: I trust Aphrodite has not heard of this for she hasn't said a word.

Hermes: She has been far away and returned just late last night. It won't be long before she hears the worst.

Aphrodite: [entering from left] Who hears what? What are you talking about? Is it a secret? I love secrets.

Hermes: Well, you won't like this one.

Aphrodite: Try me.

Hermes: [shrugging] On earth there lives a very beautiful princess named Psyche. She is the youngest of three daughters born to the king and queen of Miletus. She is exquisite. Unfortunately, the people in her country and also from afar have decided that she is really you. Hence they are worshiping her and have abandoned your temples. [Aphrodite starts pacing back and forth] I am afraid it is a serious problem.

Aphrodite: [turning abruptly] The tramp! I'll make her wish that she was never born. You watch. [goes to exit right and calls out] Eros, Eros, come here.

Eros: [entering right] Yes, Mother. [swinging his bow and arrow]

Aphrodite: I need your help. You are always using that bow and arrow. I don't know how you will use it on this job but you can figure it out. I have something important, very important for you to do for me.

Eros: But Mother, you have always said that I am full of mischief. Do you think I am capable of doing something important?

Aphrodite: Stop trying my patience. Can't you see that I am angry? Now listen. I want you to find a girl called Psyche, who is beautiful but is passing herself off as me. Can you imagine? People are paying homage to her. They follow her around. Very few are going to my temples. In fact the temples are falling into disrepair. You find that girl and make sure that no one falls in love with her. See that she falls in love with something monstrous and evil.

Eros: This sounds like mischief to me.

[curtain]

SCENE 3. A hilltop in Miletus.

The king and queen, and Psyche are standing on precipice.

Narrator: [standing in front of curtain] In the meantime the king and queen, parents of Psyche, arrived at the oracle of Apollo. After making sacrifices and offering gifts they asked advice from the oracle. They specifically asked what man their daughter would marry. The oracle, having promised to help Eros, answered that Psyche would have no mortal lover, but would marry a serpent, a hideous monster. The parents were to prepare Psyche for the wedding by dressing her as for a funeral. They were then to take her to a high precipice where she was to await alone for her bridegroom. The parents naturally were distraught.

[curtain]

King: [sobbing] My dear daughter, Psyche. It grieves your mother and I so to leave you here alone but it is what the oracle commanded. We dare not go against his wishes.

Psyche: Father, I am not afraid. Please dry your tears. I will be all right.

Queen: [embracing Psyche] Sweet gentle girl. I will always remember with joy your lovely face. I cannot bear to think about your future.

Psyche: Mother, please, spare yourself. I am truly not frightened. I will just rest here until my bridegroom comes for me. Go now. It will be easier.

King: [to his wife] Come now. Let us go. [exits right to sound of wailing voices and drum beats]

Psyche: Now that I am alone, I feel some fear. What does it mean that my husband shall be a monster? I am terrified. On one hand I do not want to panic, I want to be in control. And yet on the other hand I want to throw myself down this cliff. [she kneels and prays to any god that will hear her] Please help me. I am little more than a child and know not the world. Please take care of me. I did not mean to offend Aphrodite.

Zephyr: [enters from left and places his hand on Psyche's cheek] My poor little Psyche, do not worry. I will waft you across the valley to the most beautiful palace. You will be surprised at the luxury of it. It is sumptuous beyond your dreams.

Psyche: Your touch seems kind. Who are you? Are you my bridegroom?

Zephyr: I am Zephyr, the west wind sent to bring you to the palace. There you will be treated with every courtesy.

Psyche: Did my bridegroom send you?

Zephyr: I am not at liberty to answer, but I will tell you that you will sleep and when you awaken, you will be on a beautiful green lawn surrounded by flowers. Nearby, water will cascade over a rocky creek bed and behind all of this will be a stately palace, shimmering in the sun as though inlaid with jewels.

Psyche: This all sounds like a fairy tale. Will I be happy there? Will my family be able to visit me?

Zephyr: Just put your head down and go to sleep and then we will be away. That is good. Just close those eyes. [Psyche goes to sleep]

[curtain]

SCENE 4. The palace.

[curtain]

Narrator:	So Psyche awakened as expected. She arose and went into the palace. Voices talked to her there, but she saw no one. She bathed and dressed, ate a delicious dinner, and still saw no one. The days passed, one after another, and Psyche forgot to think of the dreaded bridegroom. One night she stood on the balcony overlooking the gardens, thinking of her family and feeling rather lonely, when a voice spoke to her.
Voice:	[reassuring] Do not be afraid, Psyche. I constantly have my eyes upon you.
Psyche:	Who are you?
Voice:	I am your husband. My love for you is not in the plans of the gods, but when I first saw you I knew you were to be my wife.
Psyche:	You are my husband?
Voice:	Yes, dear Psyche. It was I who sent the West Wind for you. It was I who had this lovely palace built for you.
Psyche:	Then you cannot be the monster I was promised for my spouse.
Voice:	No, Psyche. You must believe me. You must trust me. You will not see me but I will take care of you. Do not try to see me. Just trust me.

[dim lights for a few seconds]

Psyche:	Today my sisters call to me. I hear them crying from atop the precipice. I have not answered, but they call and call. Please may I answer them. They call out that they wonder what has happened to me.
Voice:	No, Psyche. It will be the end of our happiness. Do not ask it.
Psyche:	[weeping] But I have no happiness when I think of my sisters out there on the ledge weeping for me.
Voice:	I don't like it but I'll give it a try. I'll have the West Wind bring them tomorrow. But mind, Psyche, you must never ask my name nor seek to see my face.

[dim lights for a few seconds]

Psyche:	Dear sisters, please come into my home. [enter two sisters from left; the sisters embrace]

Sister #1: [looking around with amazement on her face] I can't believe this palace. I can't believe how we got here. We were sitting on the cliff and suddenly we seemed to be lifted right through the air. It was like we were riding on a magic carpet.

Sister #2: So here we are. This place is marvelous. But the terrible bridegroom? What of him, dear sister?

Psyche: Oh, he is no monster, but the fairest prince imaginable, quite young and very handsome. You girls sit down and I will go to see to refreshments. [exits left]

Sister #2: So our sweet little Psyche lives in such splendor. She seems to be a goddess. This whole thing is unsettling.

Sister #1: Yes, I agree. Who does she think she is?

Psyche: [returning] Dear sisters, it is so good to see you. The wine and cakes will be here in a moment.

Sister #2: This monster, I mean this husband of yours, dear sister, what is his age?

Psyche: He is much older than I, oh, I mean he is not so much older than I and he is quite young and handsome, but maybe he is a little older than I.

Sister #1: [whispers to sister #2] What is her problem? I don't think she has ever seen him. See how she trips herself up.

Sister #2: All that he has done for you, this palace, the beautiful clothes, and jewelry are designed to ease your apprehension. When you least expect it, he will pounce. [to sister #1] We must convince her that he is indeed a menace. Why should she have all this luxury?

Sister #1: If he is all that you say he is, why should you not see him? From the way you talk we know that you have not seen him. Why is this? There must be a reason and we can't think of one good one. So it must be an evil reason. So tell me, why is this?

Psyche: He truly loves me. I know it. Why do you question me so?

Sister #2: Do not answer a question with a question. You are evading the issue, which is why haven't you seen him?

Sister #1: Will you admit that you have not seen him?

Psyche: (voice quavering) Did you know that my husband arranged for your visit here?

Sister #2:	You're still trying to get me off the subject. And you still have not answered my question.
Psyche:	[sobbing] You are right. I have not seen him. I do not know why I cannot see him but I know he loves me.
Sister #2:	[puts her arm around Psyche] Now that's better. Now we are getting somewhere. I want you to find out who your husband is before it is too late.
Psyche:	Too late for what?
Sister #2:	Come now! You know what I mean. If he is a monster we want you to know about it so that you can protect yourself. We will help you. So find out who your husband really is.
Psyche:	Yes, I understand. I am to find out who my husband really is.
Sister #2:	Psyche has come to her senses. Please arrange our ride back to the cliff. And it was good to see you, dear. [sisters exit right]

[curtain]

SCENE 5: Palace bedroom.

[curtain]

Narrator:	Poor Psyche! Her sisters exhibit some type of superior control of her. So against her own better judgment she decided to see what her husband looked like. In the night she sneaked into the bedroom where he was sleeping. In bending over to gaze upon his countenance, she dropped a bit of oil from the lamp. It was enough to awaken her beloved.
Eros:	[springing from the bed] Psyche! Where is your faith? You will hate yourself when you know the truth. I am Eros, son of Aphrodite. Aphrodite asked me to find for you some hideous husband. Can you guess what happened?
Psyche:	Yes, I think I know. You fell in love with me.
Eros:	Yes, dear Psyche. I fell in love with you. The very moment I first saw you, I drew an arrow from my quiver and accidently wounded myself upon it. For the first time I, Eros, fell in love.
Psyche:	But tell me, why can't you continue to love me?

Eros: My heart is torn. I will never see you again. Love and trust go together. Where there is no trust, there is no love. [he exits left]

Psyche: [to the audience] Eros, god of love, was my husband and I, so full of pride, lost my faith and trust in him. If only I had not listened to my sisters. They bore me nothing but ill will and I did not see it. Please Eros, I love you. Come back to me.

[curtain]

Act II. The search.

Narrator: In the meantime, Aphrodite heard the news that her son Eros was ill from a wound probably incurred by an encounter with a mortal. The goddess went into a towering rage. She returned to the palace at Mount Olympus and had Eros locked up in her apartment with guards to stand watch at the door night and day. She then sent word to the other gods that Psyche had to be found and brought to justice. They were loath to cross her and were extremely troubled to find out that Psyche had sought sanctuary in a temple.

SCENE 1. The temple.

[curtain]

Psyche: [walking with great weariness enters temple from left] If I am helpful and clean up this temple maybe the god will take pity on me. [she begins to sort the material she finds on the floor]

Demeter: [entering from right] Run for your life child. Aphrodite seeks to put the seal of doom upon you. You really have her going.

Psyche: Let me hide here, great Demeter. I am so afraid and so tired.

Demeter: Child, I wish that I could. I know what it is like to be looking for someone you love and it is a terrible feeling. It seems so hopeless.

Psyche: Please, dear goddess, Demeter.

Demeter: I must not defy my own kind, though my heart aches for you. [exits right; Psyche exits left]

[dimmed lights for a few seconds]

Narrator: Poor Psyche. She stumbled out of the temple, and looking down into the valley she saw what looked like another temple. It was half hidden among the trees. She made her way down to it.

[lights brighten]

Psyche: [enters from left] This temple is Hera's. I see her name richly engraved on the altar. [she throws herself to her knees and prays] Hera, wife of the king of gods, please hear me. I am beside myself with sorrow and guilt.

Hera: [enters from right] Why do you seek help from me? Aphrodite, too, is a goddess and we do not take sides against each other. With all speed get out of here. She seeks to annihilate you.

Psyche: [walks to downstage center and faces audience] Aphrodite seeks to get rid of me but it is probable that I may find Eros in her palace ... I will ask her for mercy. What if she hurts me or even kills me? I am lost. Worse than that I am dead without my husband.

[curtain]

SCENE 2. The palace of Aphrodite.

[curtain]

Aphrodite is pacing when she is interrupted by loud knocking.

Aphrodite: Who is at the door? [sees Custom with Psyche] So you have found Psyche? Bring her in.

Custom: Yes, I found her sneaking around the place and I recognized her right off. I dragged her here. However, I'll admit she didn't try to escape.

Aphrodite: I'll reward you well, Custom. You may leave. [Custom bows his way out] Now, what do you have to say for yourself?

Psyche: I humbly offer to be your servant. I throw myself on your mercy.

Aphrodite: [laughs aloud] Ah, ha! I see the wicked creature who would take my son and take my place at my own altars! And you want to be treated as a daughter? Great! [goes to exit right and calls out] Sorrow and Anxiety come in here immediately. [enter two gray-clad figures] I want you to stay with Psyche at all times and be her servant. Yes, that's it. Be her servant. [to the audience] The other gods can't say I am being unkind to her if I give her servants. Right? [to the two gray-clad figures] Never leave her or you'll regret it.

Psyche: How is Eros? Could you just tell me ...

Aphrodite: [interrupting] Tell you about Eros? Isn't it enough that you almost killed him? What kind of a wife are you? I'll tell you one thing. You are a miserable looking creature. I've heard about your great beauty but I don't see any beauty. I see a plain girl who can't even get a husband without some sort of chicanery. That's what I see. So now you want to be my servant. Fine. I'll put you right to work. Come over here. Do you see these heaps of wheat, corn, and beans, all mixed together?

Psyche: Yes, goddess, I see them quite clearly even though my eyes are almost blinded by tears.

Aphrodite: Separate these seeds and grains. Get it done before nightfall, when I shall return from a banquet given by Zeus and Hera. Get on with it. Don't be slow. [exits right]

Psyche: Where shall I begin? I can't do this by myself. It is impossible. Please gods hear me. In your hearts pity me, the princess who has accidentally incurred the wrath of one of you. [disconsolately she sits down with her head in her hands]

[lights dim]

Narrator: Ah, but who was watching this sad scene but a colony of ants. Yes, ants. They decided to help Psyche because she too was a daughter of earth as were they. They came in droves and in straight rows marching as in a parade. Hurrying here and there among the grain and seeds, they swiftly divided them. When all was accomplished they disappeared. [Sorrow and Anxiety stand with bowed heads]

[lights brighten]

Aphrodite: [enters, sees that Psyche's task is done] Well, I see you got help, probably from Eros. I'll soon put a stop to that. Sorrow and Anxiety, you'll lose your jobs if this kind of thing happens again.

Psyche: [to the audience] So Eros knows that I am here. That makes me happy.

Aphrodite: You should be up to another job, since you are apparently an expert organizer. Across the river lies a lovely green pasture. Contained in the fenced area are wild sheep. Get me a goodly amount of their heavenly golden fleece.

[curtain]

SCENE 3. On top of a tower.

Psyche is standing stage left as if looking out from a high tower.

[curtain]

Narrator:	Poor Psyche. She was again pitted against the impossible. Or so she thought. She took herself down by the river bank and pushing the brush apart searched for the wild sheep. She heard a voice coming from a reed. She was told to wait until the sheep were finished grazing for the day and departed the area. She could then steal across the river and pick the fleece off the thickets where most certainly there would be plenty. And she did just that. She then had to collect water from a dangerous waterfall but as you might have guessed she got help here too. An eagle flew by her and taking the pouch to be filled, flew to the falls and returned it full of water. By this time Aphrodite was really annoyed. So she sent her to the Underworld to ask Persephone for a box of beauty materials.
Psyche:	[to the audience] This will be the quickest way for me to get to the Underworld. I will just throw myself off the tower and that will take care of the trip.
Voice of the Tower:	What are you thinking, little one? You have been so brave and so full of daring, surely you are not going to give up in such a manner! What a horrible way to die! And so you really want to die? If you go to the Underworld in this way you will not return. Listen to me and I will tell you what to do.
Psyche:	You want to help me?
Voice of the tower:	Yes, I do. Now give me all your attention.
Psyche:	Please go on. I am listening.
Voice of the tower:	Go to a dark cave at the end of the earth. Take two coins with you and put them between your teeth or under your tongue. Take with you some hard bread soaked a little in barley water. Take two pieces. Do not speak to anyone. There will be those who will try to get you to speak. Pay no attention. The coins are to pay for your ferry ride both coming and going. The bread is to appease Cerberus, the three-headed dog. But the biggest thing of all is the following piece of advice. Do not open the box of beauty. Under no circumstances are you to open the box.
Psyche:	Thank you sir, I do appreciate your kindness to me. I will be off.

[curtain]

SCENE 4. The Underworld.

A dark and dreary place.

[curtain]

Psyche: I will knock on this palace door.

Ghost: [wears black handkerchief over head and holds a lighted flashlight at his waist pointed at his face] Yes?

Psyche: I have come to see Queen Persephone. Please tell her that Aphrodite sent me.

Ghost: Very well. Please sit on the bench. I won't ask you in because it is too ghostly for you.

Psyche: [looking around before sitting] It is really a dreary place. I don't understand how Queen Persephone can stand it. I am told that she too was once a young girl like myself, living at home with her mother. She must hate it here.

Persephone: [enters from right] Why do you want me?

Psyche: Aphrodite sent me.

Persephone: Yes, I understand that from the ghost, but why?

Psyche: Aphrodite is so worn out and so haggard for worrying about her son Eros that her beauty is fading, or at least she thinks it is fading. She wants me to bring her some beauty from you, because you are such a beautiful goddess.

Persephone: Are you trying to flatter me?

Psyche: Of course not, I am only telling you the truth as I see it and because I've always heard it.

Persephone: Very well, I believe you. Just sit down and I will go fill the box. [Psyche gives Persephone the empty box. Persephone exits right]

Psyche: It is very strange down here. I am hungry but I must not eat the bread meant for Cerberus. Anyway, it would be hard to eat with the coin under my tongue.

Persephone: [entering from left] Take this box to Aphrodite. Do not look into it. Very well, be on your way.

[curtain]

SCENE 5. A garden.

Narrator: You must know by now that Psyche had an insatiable appetite for curiosity. She made it out of the Underworld without incident but when she saw the daylight she sat to rest and then decided she needed to freshen up and look beautiful too. So you can guess the rest. She opened the box and there was nothing in it. Well, nothing you could see. But she felt drowsy almost immediately and soon she was fast asleep.

Eros is bending over Psyche who is sleeping.

[curtain]

Eros: [kneeling and bending over Psyche] My little one. When will you learn? You have done it again. Misfortune has overtaken you again because you did not do as directed. [Psyche stirs and sits up] See what curiousity has done again, Psyche?

Psyche: Hold me dear husband. I am so afraid.

Eros: Do not be afraid. I am not going to leave you ever again.

Psyche: You are going to stay with me? You are taking me back to our beautiful palace?

Eros: No, I am going to take you with me to Mount Olympus. I have arranged this with Zeus. Come, you will meet them all, all the Olympians. There Zeus has promised me that you will be made a goddess and immortal. My mother has agreed to stop her nonsense and accept you as a lovely daughter-in-law. We will have a palace all of our own. I love you. Please trust me.

Psyche: I will always love and trust you.

[curtain]

TEACHERS' NOTES

1. Using transparency number 1, ask the students what part of the world they see. Write on the transparency: Southern Europe, Near East, North Africa, and the Mediterranean Sea. On a blank map have them lightly color all water with a light blue pencil. Using transparency number 6, have them locate Miletus on the island of Crete, Taenarus on the mainland, and Mount Olympus.

2. In reality this is more a fairy tale than a myth.[1] It appears in mythology books, and Eros is usually given the Roman name, Cupid. I decided to keep Roman names out of this book, hence I used the name Eros.

VOCABULARY

annihilate. to destroy completely

arrogant. overbearingly proud, no feeling for what others desire

chicanery. the use of tricky talk or acts to fool others

disconsolately. so sad and unhappy that nothing comforts

droves. moving crowd

evading. to keep away from or avoid by using tricks or cleverness

encounter. to come up against

incurred. to bring something (usually bad) upon oneself

inlaid. set into a surface in small pieces but leaving a smooth surface

insatiable. always wanting more, greedy

menace. a threat or danger

pitted. to match or set up against

precipice. a steep cliff that goes almost straight down

sanctuary. a place where one can find safety and shelter

shimmering. to shine with an unsteady, wavering light

sumptuous. costly, lavish

ACTIVITIES

1. Have students write their own ending beginning with Eros saying: "Where there is no trust, there is no love."

2. Read to the students "Beauty and the Beast." Write a comparision of the two tales.

3. Have students write letters: from Psyche to her mother and father; from Eros to Aphrodite; from Aphrodite to Eros; and from a sister to Psyche.

DISCUSSION QUESTIONS

Name_____

Psyche **Act I**

1. Why can't Psyche lead a normal life?

2. Why does Psyche's father worry about the folks worshiping his daughter?

3. Put the following in chronological order:

    ( ) Eros arranges for Zephyr to bring sisters for a visit.

    ( ) Sisters visit Psyche.

    ( ) Zephyr wafts Psyche to palace.

    ( ) Parents leave Psyche on precipice.

    ( ) Psyche dresses as if for a funeral.

    ( ) Psyche drops oil on her husband's face.

    ( ) Aphrodite calls Psyche a tramp.

    ( ) King visits his oracle.

4. Does Psyche seem to be brave or cowardly? Give evidence to support your opinion.

5. What character defect do you see in Psyche's sisters?

6. If you were Psyche, how would you have handled your sisters?

7. Do you think Psyche got what she asked for? Explain.

8. Research creation according to the Greek myths.

Name_____

Psyche Act II

1. How did Demeter treat Psyche?

2. Who does Aphrodite say probably helped Psyche sort the grains?

3. Do you think it was smart of Psyche to go directly to Aphrodite?

4. Why wouldn't it have been a good idea for Psyche to throw herself off the tower?

5. What specific instructions does the tower give to Psyche?

6. When Queen Persephone gives Psyche the box, do you think she is testing Psyche?

7. What character trait causes Psyche trouble?

8. Rewrite this story setting it in modern times. Your heroine, Psyche, is about fifteen years old and instead of being the daughter of a king and queen, she is the daughter of parents similar to yours. Write a brief summary of your plot.

TESTS

Name_____

Psyche **Test Yourself**

Choose the correct word from the list below and fill in the blanks.

precipice	question	carpet	chicanery
curiosity	ants	thicket	Apollo
Eros	servant	Demeter	Zephyr
Hera	monster	oil	love
Custom	Sorrow	Persephone	temple

1. _____Consulted by the king and queen about their daughter's marriage possibilities.

2. _____Psyche was to be dressed as for a funeral and left here.

3. _____Name of the West Wind.

4. _____Accidentally shot himself and fell in love.

5. _____Psyche's parents thought she would be marrying this.

6. _____Sisters felt they rode on this.

7. _____A sister said that Psyche should not answer a question with this.

8. _____Psyche dropped this on Eros.

9. _____Eros said that for the first time he experienced this.

10. _____Psyche sought sanctuary here.

11. _____Who told Psyche that Aphrodite sought to put the seal of doom upon her?

12. _____This goddess told Psyche that goddesses did not take sides against each other.

13. _____A grim person who grabbed Psyche and took her to Aphrodite.

14. _____Psyche asked Aphrodite to let her be this.

15. _____Aphrodite said Psyche was a plain girl who couldn't get a husband without some sort of this.

16. _____They came in long lines, as in a parade, to help Psyche.

17. _____One of the two gray-clad women told to watch Psyche.

18. _____Psyche, in order to get fleece, picked it off this.

19. _____Aphrodite gave an empty box to take to this person for beauty supplies.

20. _____This is what got the best of Psyche and made her open the box of beauty supplies.

Name_____

Psyche **Final Test**

Choose the correct answer and write corresponding letter in parentheses.

( )   1.   When Psyche had to collect water from a waterfall she had the assistance of: (a) a reed (b) ants (c) an eagle.

( )   2.   Psyche was the daughter of the king and queen of: (a) Miletus (b) Ithaca (c) Colchis.

( )   3.   The wind who carried Psyche from the precipice to the palace was: (a) Zephyr (b) Boreas (c) Aeolus.

( )   4.   Eros remarked that his mother always said he was: (a) naughty (b) fresh (c) mischievous.

( )   5.   The king and queen consulted: (a) their relatives (b) Apollo (c) their two older daughters.

( )   6.   When Psyche arrived at the palace of the intended bridegroom: (a) a big reception committee awaited her (b) Eros was waiting alone (c) voices talked to her but she saw no one.

( )   7.   Psyche's bridegroom came: (a) the first night she arrived (b) after many days (c) after many months.

( )   8.   Eros told Psyche: (a) she must love him (b) she must obey him (c) she must trust him.

( )   9.   When Psyche heard her sisters crying, the sisters were: (a) atop the precipice (b) in their homes (c) in Psyche's garden.

( ) 10.   When asked if the sisters could visit Psyche, Eros answered: (a) "It will be the end of our happiness" (b) "Certainly, I'll arrange it" (c) "Why do you ask me?"

( ) 11.   The sisters thought Psyche was: (a) unhappy (b) confused (c) sick.

( ) 12.   The sisters were: (a) jealous (b) concerned (c) feeling ill.

( ) 13.   The sisters said that all good things Psyche had were designed: (a) to force her to stay (b) to confuse her (c) to ease her apprehension.

( ) 14.   The sisters convinced Psyche she must: (a) learn the truth before it was too late (b) come home with them (c) visit her oracle.

( ) 15.   In bending over to gaze upon Eros's countenance, Psyche: (a) dropped her lamp (b) dropped some oil (c) lost her balance and fell.

( ) 16.   Psyche cries that she lost her husband because she was (a) selfish (b) full of pride (c) babyish.

( ) 17.   When Aphrodite heard her son was injured she: (a) laughed uproariously (b) fell into a towering rage (c) sat silently weeping.

( ) 18.   The goddess who admitted to Psyche that she knows how it feels to look for a loved one was: (a) Hera (b) Iris (c) Demeter.

( ) 19.   Hera told Psyche that Aphrodite: (a) seeks to annihilate her (b) is really sorry for Psyche (c) will eventually get over her anger.

( ) 20.   Aphrodite said to Psyche: (a) "You're really beautiful" (b) "You're very short" (c) You're a plain girl."

MYTHO GAME

(*Persephone* and *Psyche* combined)

See instructions in chapter on general activities, page 228.

1. Name Demeter's daughter.

2. Who is Demeter?

3. Who is king of the Underworld?

4. What old witchy crone did Demeter visit?

5. Who is the queen who invited Demeter to care for her son?

6. What did Demeter say she preferred to drink when she visited Metaniera?

7. Who is Metaneira's husband?

8. Name the king of the gods.

9. What kind of vehicle did Hades use to take Persephone away?

10. Who was playing with Persephone when she was abducted?

11. What kind of flowers was Persephone picking when she was abducted?

12. Who told Demeter the truth about her daughter?

13. Where did the sun live?

14. Where was Persephone living when she was kidnapped?

15. What is the name of the baby Demeter was to take care of?

16. Hecate told Demeter to consult whom?

17. Who did Zeus send to visit Hades?

18. What kind of seed did Persephone eat?

19. What season of the year does Persephone spend in Hades?

20. Whose decision concerning Persephone does Hades have to abide by?

21. Where does Zeus live?

22. What kind of nymphs were the last to see Persephone?

23. What did Hades promise Persephone?

24. What makes Hecate happy?

25. Where did Psyche's parents leave her?

26. Who is the mother of Eros?

27. Name the man who found Psyche wandering near Aphrodite's palace.

28. Who came marching in and helped Psyche sort the grains?

29. What did Psyche spill on Eros?

30. Where did Psyche get the ram's fleece.

31. What is the name of the West Wind?

32. Who did the king and queen consult about their daughter's marriage possibilities?

33. Who accidentally shot himself with an arrow?

34. Who did Psyche's parents think she had to marry?

35. What did Eros say that he experienced for the first time in his life?

36. Where did the nymphs that played with Persephone live?

37. Aphrodite said Psyche would have to resort to this to get a husband.

38. Who was Psyche to ask for beauty supplies?

39. What got the best of Psyche and made her open the box given by Persephone?

40. Who helped Psyche collect water from a waterfall?

41. Psyche's parents were the king and queen of what place?

42. Eros remarked that his mother always said he was full of what?

43. How many sisters did Psyche have?

44. What emotion did the sisters feel toward Psyche?

45. Who was the goddess who admitted to Psyche that she knew what it was like to hunt for a loved one?

46. Name one of the two servants assigned to Psyche by Aphrodite.

47. Where did people usually worship the gods?

48. What did Psyche's sister want her to do?

49. What did Aphrodite do to Eros when she discovered he had been burned with oil?

50. What banquet was Aphrodite preparing to attend when Psyche arrived at her palace?

Persephone and *Psyche* Crossword Puzzle Clues

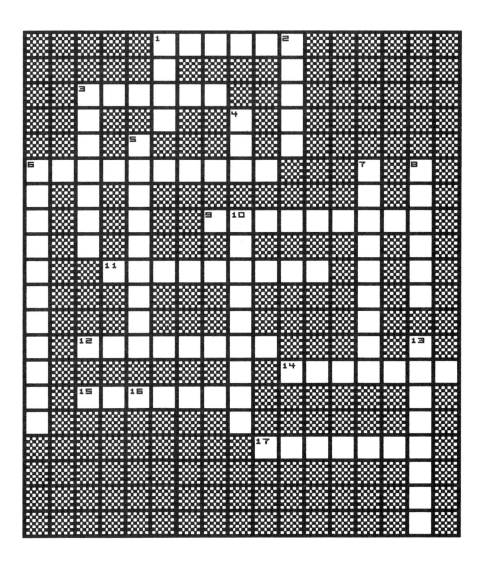

Across

1. West Wind
3. Helios dislikes this kind of day
6. Kidnapped by Hades
9. Persephone was picking these when
   she disappeared
11. He cried and fussed
12. Hades promised jewelry set with these
14. Psyche's parents lived here
15. Demeter causes this
17. Psyche, the bride, was dressed
   as for this

Down

1. He said "compromise is in order"
2. Persephone pulled flowers up by this
3. Sun god drives this
4. He knew where Persephone was
5. She asked Demeter to take care
   of her baby
6. Persephone ate the seed of this
7. Hecate is happy when she is this
8. He brought Psyche to Aphrodite
10. She hated Psyche
13. When Persephone picked the flowers,
    this is what she heard

NOTES

1. H. J. Rose, *A Handbook of Mythology*, (New York: Dutton, 1959), 287.

Daedalus

THE PLAY

Cast of Characters
In Order of Appearance

Minos, king of Crete
Adviser, nobleman of Crete
Servant, in the king's palace
Daedalus, architect of the labyrinth
Guard, member of the palace guard
Icarus, son of Daedalus
Guard, at the labyrinth
Cocalus, king of Sicily

Act 1. Treason.

SCENE 1. A room in the palace of Minos of Crete.

King Minos and his adviser are talking earnestly.

[curtain]

Narrator: We learned in the adventures of Theseus that Daedalus, architect of the infamous labyrinth in Crete, informed Ariadne, the king's daughter, how Theseus could escape from it. Minos knew at once who engineered the escape.

Minos: I am outraged. This is treason. Only one man could have told Theseus how to get out and that has to be Daedalus.

Adviser: But why are you so sure of this?

Minos: For goodness sake, think man. He is the only one who would know how because he was the trusted architect. When I wanted to build the maze, I sent out word that I wished a clever architect to design and oversee the construction. [voice rising] When I think about the treachery, I could ...

Adviser: [interrupting] Come now, don't get yourself in a frenzy.

Minos: Frenzy? Who is in a frenzy? It is easy for you to talk, but I am the king, the king of Crete. People look up to me and I now have visions of them laughing behind my back. Yes, laughing behind my back.

Adviser: No, No! Don't take on so. The people do not laugh at you.

Minos: Do you mean to tell me that they did not laugh when the Minotaur was born? Did they not say "Ha, ha, the king has finally got what he deserves? Is it not time that he was punished for not sacrificing the beautiful bull to Poseidon?"

Adviser: You underestimate the devotion of your people. They feel only sadness when you are upset. You set the tone. You are the pulse of the island. When you are upset, your people are restless. Please come to terms with yourself and get a hold of this problem. Let us say that Daedalus did this deed. What do you propose to do about it?

Minos: You are right. What am I going to do? Take action. [to servant who has been standing at attention at door right] See that Daedalus is brought to me at once. Find him. [servant exits right] I'll show you what I'll do. He will suffer in his own maze.

Adviser: That seems like a suitable punishment. He built the maze; now he can get into it. But if he could tell Theseus how to get out couldn't he get out himself?

Minos: No, he could not. I'll see that he goes in blindfolded and has nothing with him. He will be led around and around plus back and forth before being abandoned. He will never find his way out.

Adviser: If you say so. But remember, he was smart enough to design this maze; he may be just smart enough to find his way out.

Minos: Hogwash! You are trying to provoke me. Besides it was in the contract that the maze was to be so difficult that even the architect wouldn't be able to figure out the exit.

Adviser: No, I am not trying to provoke you, only trying to make you realistic. Daedalus is clever.

Minos: Well, he wasn't too clever this time. He left clues all over the place. For example, I know that he visited my daughter, Ariadne, the day before Theseus escaped from the labyrinth. And I know that Theseus visited my daughter. What conclusions am I to draw from this?

Adviser: That Ariadne had two guests. Are you saying that there is a connection?

Minos: You are the dreamer. Of course there is a connection. Daedalus visits Ariadne. Theseus visits Ariadne. Theseus escapes from the labyrinth. And then Ariadne disappears. I say Theseus was helped by Ariadne and Daedalus, and then Theseus carried off my daughter. I will avenge this treason.

Servant: [entering from right] I have Daedalus outside, Minos.

Minos: Send him in; bring him in; do whatever is necessary.

Servant: He will come in on his own accord, your royal highness. [exits]

Daedalus: [entering from right] Your royal highness, what is it that brings such a message of haste? I dropped everything and came at once. Fortunately I wasn't too far ...

Minos: Don't bother with the pretentions. I know and you know that you helped Theseus get out of the labyrinth. What have you to say for yourself, if anything?

Daedalus: Actually, there is nothing to say. You are correct. My head told me not to do so, but my heart took control and I helped them.

Minos: What do you mean, them? Tell me.

Daedalus: Ariadne was in love with Theseus and so I helped Theseus by giving instructions that he was to enter the labyrinth after tying a piece of thread to the outside door and then carrying the ball of thread with him. He could then find his way out by following the thread.

Minos: So that is how you did it! Well you will pay for it, and pay well. My darling daughter is gone. Now you will be gone. You will see how it feels to be so treated. With your son, Icarus, you will be confined in the labyrinth for all your days. [to servant] Call the guard.

Daedalus: I will not beg for mercy for myself. But what did Icarus do to you? He is innocent. My son is young.

Minos: And so too, is my daughter.

Guard: [enters from right] At your service, your majesty.

Minos: Take this man and lock him up. Find his son Icarus and lock him up, too. There will be complete instructions tomorrow. [exit guard and Daedalus] He will regret every breath he ever took.

[curtain]

SCENE 2. Inside the labyrinth.

Daedalus and Icarus sit on the floor.

[curtain]

Icarus:	Father, I still don't understand what I am doing here, or rather what we are doing here.
Daedalus:	Son, Minos is having his revenge because I helped his daughter Ariadne. She fell in love with Theseus. It was as though Eros had hit her with an arrow. When she saw Theseus marching down the street with the Athenians that were to be fed to the Minotaur, she lost her heart to him. Against my better judgment I helped her plan an escape. Theseus escaped taking the Athenians and Ariadne with him. They sailed that very night. So that, my dear son, is why we are languishing in the labyrinth of my own making.
Icarus:	You really don't seem too upset by it, so I'll follow your cue and not be upset either.
Daedalus:	Good boy! If we are calm we can think of a way. [laughs] One thing, this maze must be really good if the architect can't find his way out. I couldn't tie a thread on the door like Theseus did because the guards were on to that and they watched me closely. I have only my wits, but my wits have never let me down yet. I always think I must be related to Odysseus, he of the lively wits. We would get along famously if we should ever meet.
Icarus:	I have faith in you, Father.
Daedalus:	[rising] Come, let us check this out. The floor is solid, the walls go up straight. They are carefully joined. [shouting] I have it. Listen to me. The air and the sky. That's it. We shall fly out.
Icarus:	But how, Father? We have no wings.
Daedalus:	Where is the faith in me that you just proclaimed?
Icarus:	I'm sorry, Father. So soon I doubted you.
Daedalus:	Never mind, son, I will make our wings.
Icarus:	You will make us wings and I will learn to fly?
Daedalus:	It will be no problem. If you listen to my instructions, you'll do just fine. But now for the wings. I will need wax and feathers, not easy things to find in a labyrinth. But then again I have faith, so the wax and the feathers will not be a problem. Come son, let us sleep now so that after we are refreshed I can get started on the wings. I'll need a little help from you. We will have to hold the wings up while the wax dries.

[curtain]

Narrator: Daedalus did a superb job on the wings and gave Icarus important instructions on flying with fabricated wings. He was told not to fly too close to the sun for fear the wax would melt. But Icarus really didn't pay attention to his father. He was just thrilled at the thought of the adventure in store for him. He did soar too high and alas, just as his father predicted his wings melted and he dropped into the sea, never to be heard from again. Saddened, his father continued on to Sicily where he was warmly greeted by King Cocalus.

[curtain]

Act II. Reprisal.

SCENE 1. Palace of Minos.

Enter King Minos, and his adviser.

[curtain]

Minos: This does it. Daedalus escaped and his son, too. [pacing] I can't believe that he managed to do it. How? When? [to servant standing by exit right] Bring his guard before me. [servant exits] I want to hear from the rascal. Was he playing or guarding? What kind of soldiers do we have? I am the king of Crete and my soldiers can't do a job for me.

Adviser: We do not have the details yet.

Minos: Well, get them. I want action. [bangs his fist on table]

Adviser: Again, don't upset yourself in this manner. We will do all that we can.

Minos: Well, do it immediately. Now.

Adviser: Of course, your majesty. [exits left]

Minos: [to audience] The labyrinth has given me nothing but pain. Poseidon gave me a magnificent bull to sacrifice to him and instead I kept it because I could not part with it. I rue the day that I made such an unwise decision. Poseidon is punishing me for my pride and selfishness.

Servant: [enters from right with two guards] Your majesty, this is the guard who was stationed at the door of the labyrinth.

Minos: How did Daedalus and Icarus escape?

Guard: Your majesty, I did not leave my post nor did I sleep. No one came in or out of the door. Perhaps Daedalus and Icarus are there but for their own reasons have kept very quiet. Maybe they are dead. No one could enter or leave while I was on duty.

Minos: Get out. Get out. [guard exits right]

Adviser: [entering from left] Your majesty, I consulted the oracle. Sit down while I tell you the news. [the king sits on a bench at left] Daedalus and Icarus flew out the top of the labyrinth and into the sky.

Minos: Flew? Are you insane? People don't fly.

Adviser: I feel loath to contradict you, your majesty, but they did fly. Daedalus constructed wings from wax and feathers for both of them. They flew off together but Icarus flew too close to the sun, and fell into the sea when his wings melted.

Minos: [stunned] This is ridiculous. You are joking.

Adviser: I am not making it up.

Minos: You are dreaming. I cannot believe this.

Adviser: Your majesty, when have I tried to fool you?

Minos: [pause] You have never tried to fool me. Still it is hard to fathom. [pause] I should have realized that Daedalus would be so clever. But wait a minute. [pause] I'll outwit him. Yes, I have just the thing. Come closer. [adviser draws near] I will proclaim everywhere that there will be a huge reward for anyone who can pull a thread through a seashell. Daedalus won't be able to resist the challenge. When he does it and the reward is claimed I will know where he is.

Adviser: Great. Very good thinking.

[curtain]

SCENE 2. Sicily. The palace of King Cocalus.

Enter King Cocalus, followed by Daedalus.

[curtain]

Narrator: Just as Minos predicted, Daedalus was interested in the exciting puzzle. This was just the kind of challenge he liked.

Daedalus: Let me think about it. A big reward for pulling a thread through this shell. There has to be a way.

Cocalus: It seems like such a silly project to me but the reward is great.

Daedalus: I've got it. Have a servant get me an ant and a thread.

Cocalus: An ant? What for?

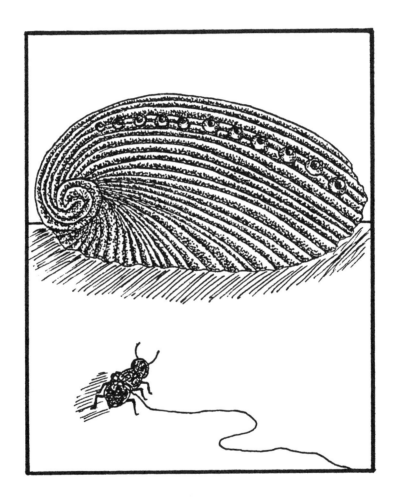

Daedalus: Don't you see? I'll bore a hole in this end of the shell, and one at the opposite end. I'll fasten the thread to the ant, lead it into the shell, and close the entry. The ant is an industrious creature and he will find his way out. When he comes out the other door, we have it, we have threaded the shell. The reward will be ours.

[curtain]

Narrator: Daedalus did just as he said. The ant did all the work for him and got nothing for his industry. Minos, however, was greatly excited as was to be expected. "We got him! We got him!" he was reported to have announced jubilantly. Minos went to Sicily to get Daedalus but the king of Sicily wouldn't hear of betraying Daedalus by turning him over to Minos. In a battle over this, Minos was killed. Daedalus lived on for many years using his inventive mind whenever the spirit moved him.

[curtain]

TEACHERS' NOTES

1. Using transparency number 1, ask the students what part of the world they see. Write on the transparency: Southern Europe, Near East, North Africa, and the Mediterranean Sea. Give the students a blank map and have them lightly color in all water a light blue. Using transparency number 7, have the students locate Sicily, Athens, and Crete.

2. The story takes place in Crete and Sicily. Daedalus, an Athenian exiled in Crete, was a master craftsman and an inventive genius. This is the same Daedalus we met in the story of Theseus.

3. Where Daedalus got the feathers and wax is never explained.

Daedalus **Transparency Master no. 7**

VOCABULARY

avenge. to get even for a wrong or injury

construct. to make or build with a plan

frenzy. a wild outburst of feeling

inventive. skilled in making something that did not exist before

loath. not willing

proclaimed. to make known publicly

rue. to feel sorry because of something

soar. to rise and fly high in the air

treachery. an act of disloyalty

treason. an act of betraying one's country

underestimate. a guess about size, ability, etc., that is too low

ACTIVITIES

1. Have the students design their own mazes. They could make the mazes as puzzles. Select the best couple of mazes, duplicate, and have a contest with the class.

2. Daedalus was an inventor. Have the students invent a tool or an appliance. Design it, name it, and, better still, explain it.

3. Research Minoan civilization, the advanced prehistoric civilization that flourished in Crete from about 3000-1000 B.C. In 1890 English archaeologist Arthur John Evans excavated the ruins in Crete and he found definite signs that Crete had indeed dated back centuries before Greece. They had internal plumbing which the Greeks never had. They also had a navy. Artwork revealed that bulls did play a big part in their religious ceremonies. The myths about Minos represent memories of an actual great civilization. Evans acknowledged the value of the myths by referring to this ancient civilization as "Minoan," which is what we have called it ever since.[1]

4. Read "Triumph of Daedalus," (*National Geographic* [August 1988] 174:191). Give a report to the class.

DISCUSSION QUESTIONS

Name_____

Daedalus Act I

1. Why does Minos think Daedalus engineered Theseus's escape?

2. Where did events of story take place?

3. Do you think Daedalus committed treason?

4. What do you think would have happened if Icarus had really listened to his father? Do you listen to your parents?

5. If you were Daedalus how would you have handled the situation when summoned to the king?

6. Why does Minos think that Poseidon is angry at him?

7. What event is pure fantasy?

8. Research Daedalus.

Name_____

Daedalus Act II

1. Put the following events in order:

    ( )   Minos discovers the whereabouts of Daedalus.
    ( )   An ant pulls a thread through the shell.
    ( )   Cocalus refuses to surrender Daedalus.
    ( )   The guard says he never left his post.
    ( )   Minos hears of the escape.
    ( )   Minos says that it is insanity to say they flew off.
    ( )   Minos says he is being punished for pride and selfishness.
    ( )   Minos yells "We got him."

2. Would you be annoyed at the guard if you were Minos?

3. How do you know that Minos is excitable?

4. What does Minos blame for all his problems?

5. How did the adviser find out that Daedalus escaped by flying?

6. How does Minos know that Daedalus will be unable to resist the challenge of pulling a thread through a shell?

7. After the death of Minos, what did Daedalus do with his life?

8. Write a letter from Daedalus to a friend in Greece recounting the recent adventure.

TESTS

Name_____

Daedalus Test Yourself

Using the words below fill in the spaces. Each word will be used once.

King Minos	Poseidon	Icarus	ant
Odysseus	labyrinth	wax	feathers
Sicily	Theseus	Daedalus	

1. _____An intricate maze.

2. _____Architect of the maze.

3. _____He couldn't understand why he was locked up in the maze.

4. _____This small creature was selected to pull a thread through a shell.

5. _____He was outraged by architect's escape.

6. _____Ariadne fell in love with him.

7. _____The architect feels he might be related to this man because he has such quick wits.

8. _____The architect says that he will need two things to build the wings.

9. _____The architect escaped and flew here.

10. _____The magnificent bull was a gift to Minos from this god.

Name_____

Daedalus **Final Test**

(　)　1.　King Minos said the only one who would know how to engineer an escape from the labyrinth would be: (a) Icarus (b) Theseus (c) Daedalus.

(　)　2.　King Minos said whoever was responsible for the escape was guilty of: (a) treason (b) espionage (c) disloyalty.

(　)　3.　King Minos said he was going to: (a) forget it (b) consult his oracle (c) take action.

(　)　4.　It was part of the contract: (a) that not even the architect would know the way out of the maze (b) that knowledge of the exit would be hidden from all but the architect (c) that knowledge of the exit would be held secret for twenty years.

(　)　5.　When King Minos demanded to see the architect: (a) it took two weeks to find him (b) he came immediately (c) he was never found.

(　)　6.　Theseus escaped from the maze and sailed for: (a) Ithaca (b) Athens (c) Ioclus.

(　)　7.　Icarus flew too near the: (a) water (b) sun (c) mountains.

(　)　8.　King Minos reacted to the news of the escape by: (a) ranting and raving (b) keeping his cool (c) sleeping.

(　)　9.　King Minos was king of: (a) Crete (b) Athens (c) Corinth.

(　)　10.　According to King Minos, Poseidon punished him for his: (a) pride and selfishness (b) lack of integrity (c) treason.

(　)　11.　Ariadne gave a ball of thread to: (a) a servant (b) Theseus (c) Theseus's servant.

(　)　12.　Icarus: (a) followed his father's advice (b) paid no attention to advice (c) asked his oracle for advice.

(　)　13.　Ariadne fell in love with Theseus when he: (a) fought the Minotaur (b) stepped off the ship (c) marched down the street with the Athenians.

(　)　14.　When Daedalus escaped he flew to: (a) Naxos (b) Sardinia (c) Sicily.

(　)　15.　King Minos: (a) thought the people were laughing at him (b) thought the people were crying because of his problems (c) never mentioned how he felt.

(　)　16.　The adviser cautioned King Minos that Daedalus was: (a) insane (b) stubborn (c) clever.

(　)　17.　Daedalus was sentenced to the labyrinth for: (a) life (b) ten years (c) twenty years.

(　)　18.　The relationship of Daedalus to Icarus was that of: (a) uncle/nephew (b) father/son (c) grandfather/grandson.

(　)　19.　Icarus: (a) was confused by why they were in the labyrinth (b) understood perfectly why they were in the labyrinth (c) said he thought the whole thing was a grave injustice.

(　)　20.　Icarus learned to (a) fly on fabricated wings (b) to climb out of labyrinth (c) to dive into sea safely.

NOTES

1. Isaac Asimov, *Words from the Myths* (Boston: Houghton-Mifflin, 1969), 92.

The Wooden Horse

THE PLAY

Cast of Characters
In Order of Appearance

Odysseus, king of Ithaca
Diomedes, nobleman
Menelaus, husband of Helen
Neoptolemus, son of Achilles
Epeius, master craftsman
Deiphobus, Trojan warrior
Antenor, Trojan warrior
Aeneas, Trojan warrior
Sinon, cousin of Odysseus
King Priam, king of Troy
Laocoön, priest
Cassandra, daughter of Priam
Helen, wife of Menelaus
Aphrodite, goddess of love and beauty

SCENE 1. In the Greek camp.

Present are Odysseus, Diomedes, Menelaus, and Neoptolemus.

[curtain]

Odysseus: Give a cheer! Let's hear it!

Men: Yea! Yea! [loud shouts of joy]

Odysseus: It is true that we were able to seize the palladium, the most sacred image of Pallas Athena. We have new hope.

Diomedes: While the Trojans had this image inside their walled city, we were doomed. We could never have conquered them. This is a new beginning.

Menelaus: Yes, I feel revitalized. We should all rejoice. We should put our heads together and think this out. The stalemate has been going on too long. We must capture Troy.

Diomedes: All our fighting leads to nowhere. We must get inside the city of Troy. [all men shake their heads in agreement and then all look at Odysseus] You, Odysseus, the sharp-witted, can come up with a plan. Surely you can.

Odysseus: Yes, you are correct in saying that we must get inside, but whether you are correct in saying that I can come up with a plan is another story. Still, I'll give it a try. The city seems as strong as ever. The walls stand intact without injury. In fact, all the fighting has taken place some distance from the city. This makes it imperative that we get inside the walls. All the fighting of the past nine years and more has not won us victory.

Neoptolemus: If we try to go over the walls, we will be targets for their arrows. If we try to sneak in at night, the gates will be locked.

Odysseus:	I have it. We will build a huge wooden horse — so big that it will hold a large number of men. Come let me show you what I have in mind. [men draw closer to Odysseus and watch him as he bends over table and sketches]
Diomedes:	All right, so we build a horse. How does this help us?
Odysseus:	Don't you see? We shall hide in it and think of some way to get the Trojans to bring the horse inside the gates.
Neoptolemus:	Excellent idea. Now let's get down to details. Who will make the horse?
Odysseus:	We have with us Epeius, who is a skilled craftsman. We will get him on it right away.
Neoptolemus:	Epeius is a skilled craftsman? I can't believe it. He is so scared of his own shadow I wouldn't think he could hold a knife or hammer.
Odysseus:	You underestimate his abilities. He may be middle-aged and actually not the most handsome fellow in the world, but he does have talent. That he seems frightened is true. But there is something in his background which makes him that way, I am sure. But we are not concerned with all that. We want him to build a wooden horse and that he can do. Believe me.
Neoptolemus:	I believe you, Odysseus. It is just that Epeius just doesn't seem to have it.
Odysseus:	Youth can be hard on an older generation. Take it easy. Give him a chance. He will be pleased to have his ability recognized and will work with speed and care. Neoptolemus, would you go outside and have word sent to Epeius that I want to see him at once. [Neoptolemus exits left] Once the horse is completed some of us will hide in the horse.
Menelaus:	I don't want to seem a coward but I don't think this plan is feasible. It will only end in tragedy. If this is so I will never see my wife Helen.
Odysseus:	Think positively.
Diomedes:	I, too, think it is risky. Perhaps we should give it more thought. I really wouldn't want to be in that horse.
Odysseus:	Forget it. You people told me to come up with a plan and now you are backing out before I have even started. Now listen to me. My plan is this: We shall take about eighteen men in the horse with us. All the others will be aboard the ships which the Trojans will see moving out to sea, but the ships will pull beyond the nearest island and hide. They will wait there until the men see that the horse is inside the city. If something goes wrong, the ships can head out to the high seas and home.

Menelaus:	But what about those in the horse?
Odysseus:	I've thought of that. Sinon will stay behind. He will pretend to be devastated because we left without him. He is most persuasive on any subject. We have nothing to worry about.
Neoptolemus:	[entering from left] So what have you decided?
Odysseus:	We will have about eighteen men in the horse.
Neoptolemus:	Count me in.
Menelaus:	Youth! Oh, to be young again! You are your father's son.
Odysseus:	Yes, Achilles would be proud of you. You will be in the horse. You are the first one to show enthusiasm for the idea.
Diomedes:	My enthusiasm is there, but somewhat dimmed by the thought of the big risk involved.
Epeius:	[entering from left] Did you wish to speak to me, Odysseus?
Odysseus:	Come in, Epeius, I have a big job for you. Come close while I explain the job and show you my design.

[dim lights for twenty seconds]

Odysseus:	Very good. Then it is settled. Epeius, take as many men as you wish to help you. One very important factor is speed. So get with it.
Epeius:	Right, royal leader, I will get started immediately, but I beg you not to assign me to be in the horse. I could not bear it.
Odysseus:	Do you think it will not be safe? Would your structure be weak? What ails you, man?
Epeius:	I live in fear. You know this.
Odysseus:	We'll discuss this later.
Epeius:	[exiting left] Yes, royal master. I'll get started on the project.
Diomedes:	[to Odysseus] So what exactly is our plan? Let us go over it again.

Odysseus: Some of us will hide in the wooden horse which under the cover of night will be set outside the gates of Troy. The others will take the ships and go out to sea, anchoring just beyond Tenedos. We will leave Sinon in the deserted Greek camp to be discovered by the Trojans. He is so persuasive that I feel confident that he will convince Priam that we Greeks gave up and went home. Once the Trojans have pulled the wooden horse into the city, and all the Trojans are quiet for the night, we will lower ourselves from the trap door and charge the unsuspecting enemy.

[curtain]

SCENE 2. The deserted Greek camp.

Enter Deiphobus, Antenor, and Aeneas.

[curtain]

Deiphobus: This place is cleaned out. Burned to the ground. I saw the flames and smoke last night but I didn't dare come out to investigate. I thought perhaps the enemy was deliberately trying to draw us into battle. [pauses, looks around] It rather looks like they left in haste. I see here a cloak and here a quiver.

Antenor: Yes, it looks as though they did absent themselves without much preparation. Here are the remains of a meal. What could be the meaning of this?

Deiphobus: Come over here. This must have been the tent of Odysseus. A spy told me that it was situated right next to the riverbank and set among the trees.

Antenor: I learned too, that his tent had a great view of the sea, and over here I believe was where Agamemnon had his tent. According to my spies, Achilles' tent was here. This is where he did the major part of his sulking. It is a pity that when his mother was trying to make him invulnerable that she held him by the heel. Of course he was an enemy so I shouldn't really care, but I've often wondered if we had met under different circumstances whether or not we would have been friends.

Deiphobus: What circumstances could be more honorable than war?

Antenor: Try not to get into a philosophical discussion. We are out here looking for evidence about the Greeks. One thing is certain. They have left and they left in haste.

[enter Aeneas with Sinon staggering behind him]

Aeneas: We found this fellow behind that huge wooden horse, behaving in a most furtive manner. Stand up straight fellow and tell us who you are.

Sinon: Please spare me. Don't kill me. I beg you, spare my life.

Deiphobus: Why don't you take him to Priam? Let the king decide what to do with him. Mind you, don't let him go.

[curtain]

SCENE 3. Courtyard of Priam's palace.

Present are Priam, Sinon, Antenor, Cassandra, and Laocoön.

[curtain]

Priam: Stop the sniffling. Stand up like a man.

Sinon: But the Greeks all went away and left me. I was chosen to expiate the sins of the Greeks.

Priam: Expiate for what?

Sinon: [sobbing] Pallas Athena was very angry when Odysseus and Diomedes stole the Palladium. She said she had been dishonored.

Priam: So speak up quickly. What happened?

Sinon: Odysseus sent a man to visit the oracle and he came back with the news that one of us must be sacrificed and then the Greeks should head for home.

Priam: Yes, but why are you left alone here?

Sinon: The sacrificial rites were to be held just before they sailed away, but I escaped in the night and hid in a nearby ravine. Please spare me. I meant no harm to you. I have been betrayed by my own. Let the enemy show mercy.

Priam: Your story touches me. [pause] I believe you. Henceforth, you shall have no worries. You will be known as one of us. But tell me, why the wooden horse?

Sinon: That horse was made as an offering to Pallas Athena.

Priam: But why the size?

Sinon: Ah, your highness, that was so that you Trojans could not take it into the city. You see the Greeks hoped you would destroy it and bring down the wrath of Athena upon yourselves.

Priam:	So that is it!
Laocoön:	I would tread carefully here. Something does not seem quite right to me. I fear the Greeks even when they bear gifts.
Cassandra:	I agree with you, Laocoön. There is something not quite right about this story.
Priam:	We are not interested in what you have to say, Cassandra. I don't know why you keep offering suggestions when you are well aware that no one will pay attention to a thing you say. Just go to your room and stay there and let the men handle this situation.
	[curtain]
Narrator:	Poor Laocoön. No sooner had he spoken, when a dreadful serpent came up from the sea and glided straight to Laocoön. Wrapping his huge coils around Laocoön, he crushed the life out of him. The assembly watched in horror as the serpent slithered away, disappearing into Athena's temple.

SCENE 4. Inside the horse.

Present are Odysseus, Diomedes, Neoptolemus, Epeius, and Menelaus.

[curtain]

Odysseus:	[speaking in stage whispers] Can you hear anything from the outside?
Diomedes:	[ear to the trap door] Just barely. They seem to be arguing on how to move us.
Odysseus:	That is news. That tells us that the Trojans believed Sinon's story and that we are going to be brought inside the gates. I feel some movement now. Hang on, men.
Neoptolemus:	Shh-shh, I hear them now. They are trying to decide how to get us through the gate. It is too narrow.
Odysseus:	Where is Epeius? I told him to sit by the trapdoor. I can't believe this. That fellow is impossible.
Diomedes:	He is hiding over in a corner. Why did we bring him anyway? He is such a coward, but I suppose he cannot help it.
Odysseus:	Since he designed the trapdoor, I thought it better for him to work it. Epeius, get up here and be a man.

Epeius:	Sir, if you please, I can hardly move, I am so full of fright.
Odysseus:	Don't stand. Just crawl over by that trapdoor and stay there.
Neoptolemus:	[putting his ear to wall] The Greeks have decided to take the gates off and shave a small portion from the wall and then rehang the gates.
Odysseus:	Get as comfortable as you can men. We will be here awhile. Pass the pouch of water around. I am sure we could all use some. It is mighty hot in here.
Diomedes:	Did anybody bring any wine? Well, what a pity. Did anybody think to bring food? Food is an important part of my lifestyle.
Menelaus:	Talking about it will not help.

[dim lights for a few seconds]

Odysseus:	All right men! This is it. The horse has not been moved in many hours. The sounds of revelry have ceased. Any time now Sinon will give the signal to open the trapdoor.
Menelaus:	I am still worried about the outcome of all this. My mind drifts from thoughts about Helen, long held captive by the Trojans, to problems we face right now.
Odysseus:	I hear a faint rap on the trapdoor. Epeius, open the trapdoor slowly. (Epeius reluctantly opens door and Odysseus peers out) Yes, it is Sinon. Rejoice!
Narrator:	The Greeks slipped out of the horse and immediately opened the gates of the city. The Greek army moved in silently and lit fires all over the city. Troy was almost completely destroyed before the citizens were fully awake. The Trojans had celebrated too much too soon.

[curtain]

SCENE 5. Helen's sitting room in the Trojan palace.

Present are Helen and Aphrodite.

[curtain]

Helen:	[weeping] My dear husband will be killed. It is so many years since I have seen him. I don't know what to do. [wringing her hands]

Aphrodite: You must stop carrying on in this manner. You did the best you could under the circumstances. I do not think Menelaus will be killed. The war is almost over. In fact, It is over and very soon you will be reunited with your husband. I am sure that he knows you still love him and that your being here was not of your doing.

Helen: Do you think he knows I tried to help the Greeks? Odysseus, when he sneaked in here for the Palladium, knew that I recognized him. But I said nothing.

Aphrodite: Menelaus is not stupid. However, he is angry, but he will get over it. So stop this crying.

Helen: You are right. I must get myself together.

Aphrodite: Now quickly get your things. Get a cloak; it will be cold outside. Come quickly.

Helen: Thank you for helping me. I know my husband will repay you when all is over.

Aphrodite: Your husband always thanks the gods. And Helen, you must not forget to worship at my temple.

Helen: I will not forget, gracious goddess.

Narrator: And so Aphrodite helped in the reunion of Helen and Menelaus. When the morning came, what was once the glorious city of Troy lay smoldering from fires set by Greeks. The stories differ as to how many Trojan men survived the massacre, but we do know that Aeneas and Antenor did escape. The Trojan women were taken into captivity as slaves. The Greeks left victoriously but not without problems. Odysseus, as you already know, took ten years to reach Ithaca.

[curtain]

TEACHERS' NOTES

1. Using transparency number 1, ask students what part of the world they see. Write on the transparency: Southern Europe, Near East, North Africa, and the Mediterranean Sea. Give them each a blank map and have them color the water a light blue. Using transparency number 8, have them locate Troy and the island, Tenedos. Using transparency number 3, have them locate Ithaca and Sparta.

2. The Trojan War was at a stalemate for nine years. Homer's *Illiad* is a detailed account of that final year. An oracle told the Greeks that they could not win as long as the Trojans held the Palladium, the revered statue of Athena. Odysseus and Diomedes sneaked into Troy and stole it from the Trojans. Now that they had the Palladium the Greeks felt more self-confident.

3. The stories about how Athena became Pallas Athena are varied. According to Michael Grant and John Hazel, Pallas was the playmate of Athena who was accidentally killed by the goddess. In grief, Athena put the name Pallas before her own name.[1]

4. Diomedes is not the same Diomedes spoken of in *The Golden Fleece.*

5. Cassandra had the gift of prophecy from Apollo. Apollo, annoyed at her, could not take the gift back so he willed that henceforth no one would believe her. She spoke up in *The Wooden Horse* and warned King Priam of Greek treachery but of course no one paid attention.[2]

6. "Epeius was born a coward, in divine punishment for his father's breach of faith."[3] His father had sworn in Athena's name and then reneged on a promise.

The Wooden Horse **Transparency Master no. 8**

VOCABULARY

appease. to satisfy or make calm by giving what is wanted

expiate. to make up for doing something wrong

feasible. a plan capable of being carried out

furtive. acting in a sly, sneaky way

imperative. necessary, urgent

invulnerable. cannot be hurt, destroyed, damaged

persuasive. able to persuade

plausible. seems to be true, honest, and fair, but may not be

revelry. noisy merrymaking

revitalized. to put energy back into

stalemate. a halt in a struggle because both sides are equally strong

ACTIVITIES

1. Read an account of the Trojan War. There are concise accounts in *Bulfinch's Mythology*, pages 211-36, and in Hamilton's *Mythology*, pages 178-201 (see bibliography for details).

2. Write a report on the great heroes of the Trojan War.

3. Give an oral report on some phase of the Trojan War. Perhaps it could be "The Role of Women in the Trojan War," "Famous Heroes of the Trojan War," or "The Sons of Heroes in the Trojan War." In the latter case, Achilles, Odysseus, Ajax the Greater and Ajax the Lesser, and Diomedes were all sons of heroes.

DISCUSSION QUESTIONS

Name_____

1. What did the Greeks decide to do to get into the city of Troy?

2. What revitalized the Greeks and gave them new beginnings?

3. What might have been the outcome if Priam had listened to Cassandra?

4. Put the following events in order of occurrence:

    ( ) Cassandra is sent to her room.
    ( ) Greeks are happy because they have the Palladium.
    ( ) Sinon is taken before Priam.
    ( ) Epeius is commissioned to make the wooden horse.
    ( ) City of Troy is burned.
    ( ) Greeks get into the horse.
    ( ) Epeius acts cowardly.
    ( ) Sinon is apprehended by Trojans.

5. Do you think it was right for Odysseus to leave his cousin Sinon to face the enemy alone? Why or why not?

6. Who do you most respect? Why?

7. If you were a Greek general, how would you have felled Troy?

8. Write a paragraph in which you contrast Epeius and Neoptolemus.

TESTS

Name_____

The Wooden Horse **Test Yourself**

Using words below fill in the spaces. Each word will be used once.

Sinon   Diomedes   Priam   Epeius

Palladium   Menelaus   Laocoön   Neoptolemus

Trojans   Cassandra

1._____The statue of Athena, on which the safety of Troy depended.

2._____He and Odysseus stole the statue of Athena.

3._____The son of Achilles.

4._____They worked so hard to save their city.

5._____He built the wooden horse.

6._____King who said Sinon could remain with the Trojans.

7._____He was crushed to death by a huge serpent.

8._____No one ever paid any attention to what she said.

9._____A cousin of Odysseus.

10._____His wife was rescued.

Name_____

The Wooden Horse **Final Test**

( )   1. Cassandra at one time was given the gift of prophecy. Unfortunately no one: (a) ever believed what she said (b) was ever around to hear her (c) could understand her meaning.

( )   2. The person commissioned to build the Trojan horse was: (a) Laocoön (b) Sinon (c) Epeius.

( )   3. Cassandra was given the gift of prophecy by: (a) Apollo (b) Zeus (c) Hera.

( )   4. The most sacred image of Athena was: (a) the Palladium (b) the trident (c) the palace of Athena.

( )   5. Other than Odysseus, the most enthusiastic about the wooden horse was: (a) Neoptolemus (b) Menelaus (c) Diomedes.

( )   6. Priam was: (a) head of the Greek army (b) King of Troy (c) second in command of Trojan army.

( )   7. When captured Sinon said: (a) the plan was that he be sacrificed but he escaped (b) he always wanted to be on the Trojan side (c) he told the truth, that he was purposely left in order to fool the Trojans.

( )   8. Helen was helped to escape by: (a) Athena (b) Aphrodite (c) Hera.

( )   9. A serpent sneaked into the city of Troy and crushed to death: (a) Priam (b) Laocoön (c) Diomedes.

( ) 10. The biggest coward in *The Wooden Horse* was: (a) Epeius (b) Sinon (c) Menelaus.

( ) 11. The city of Troy was destroyed by: (a) flood (b) fire (c) famine.

( ) 12. Achilles was the father of: (a) Epeius (b) Sinon (c) Neoptolemus.

( ) 13. The Greek ships withdrew to hide behind the island of: (a) Samos (b) Crete (c) Tenedos.

( ) 14. The wooden horse was big enough for about: (a) a thousand men (b) eighteen men (c) fifty men.

( ) 15. Laocoön said: (a) "This man is a good man. I believe him" (b) "I fear the Greeks even when they bear gifts" (c) "I wish the Trojans gave such gifts."

( ) 16. Aeneas found Sinon behaving in a: (a) furtive manner (b) riotous manner (c) joyful manner.

( ) 17. Antenor said Achilles did a great deal of: (a) card playing (b) praying (c) sulking.

( ) 18. Odysseus's tent in the Greek camp had a view of: (a) a deep ravine (b) the Phrygian forest (c) the sea.

( ) 19. Aphrodite told Helen that Menelaus was: (a) angry (b) disconsolate (c) happy.

( ) 20. Of the following Trojans, which one escaped at the end of the war: (a) Paris (b) Aeneas (c) Priam.

MYTHO GAME

(*Daedalus* and *The Wooden Horse* combined)

See instructions in chapter on general activities, page 228.

1. Who was the king of Crete?

2. Who was the architect of the labyrinth?

3. What princess helped Theseus escape the labyrinth?

4. What is a violation of one's allegiance toward one's country called?

5. Who gave the king of Crete the Minotaur?

6. What was the Minotaur?

7. Who flew so close to the sun that his wings melted?

8. When the architect of the labyrinth escaped where did he go?

9. Who pulled a thread through a shell?

10. Besides feathers from what did the architect of the labyrinth make wings?

11. Who is the son of Achilles?

12. What is the prized statue of Athena called?

13. Who lived in the walled city of Troy?

14. How long had the Trojan War been at a stalemate?

15. Whose idea was it to build a wooden horse?

16. Who made the wooden horse?

17. What was Epeius's profession before the war?

18. About how many men were in the wooden horse?

19. Who sat near the trapdoor in the wooden horse?

20. Who was a natural-born coward?

21. Who is referred to as "he of the lively wits"?

22. When the Greeks sailed the ships out, who was left behind to be found by the Trojans?

23. What part of Achille's body was vulnerable?

24. Who was the king of Troy during the war?

25. What men stole the Palladium from the Trojans?

26. Who was it that no one ever believed?

27. What was the name of the priest who warned Priam not to bring the wooden horse inside the gates?

28. What crushed Laocoön to death?

29. What goddess came to help Helen of Troy?

30. How was the city of Troy destroyed?

31. Other than Odysseus, who was the most enthusiastic about the wooden horse?

32. Who taught Icarus to fly?

33. What was the king of Crete supposed to do with the beautiful bull given him by Poseidon?

34. What does Daedalus say took control of him when he helped Theseus?

35. With whom did Theseus march down the streets when he arrived in Crete?

36. King Minos said Ariadne behaved as if Eros had hit her with what?

37. What was King Minos going to do to the young Athenians?

38. Daedalus said "Escape may be checked by water and land." What did that leave him?

39. Into what did Icarus drop?

40. Besides pride, for what did Minos admit he was punished?

41. Who told the king's advisers how Daedalus and Icarus escaped?

42. Where did King Minos die?

43. How did King Minos die?

44. What is the name of the king of Sicily?

45. Who was the king of Crete's adviser?

46. In what sea is the island of Crete?

47. At the tip of what country is Sicily?

48. Crete is south of what country?

49. Athens is in what country?

50. From what city did Theseus and Daedalus come?

DAEDALUS AND *THE WOODEN HORSE* CROSSWORD PUZZLE CLUES

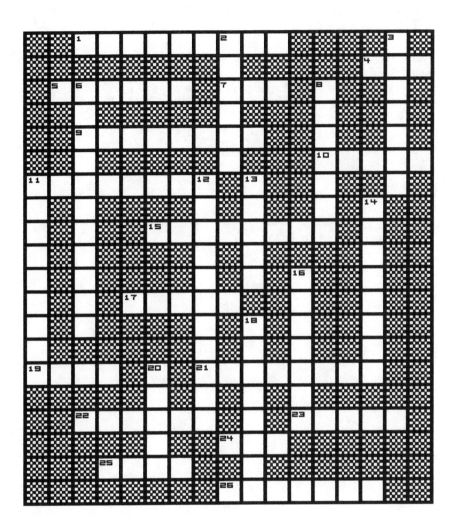

Across

1. Goddess of love and beauty.
4. Daedalus used this to make wings.
5. Daedalus flew here.
7. Used to pull thread through a shell.
9. Architect of the labyrinth.
10. Cousin of Odysseus.
11. God of the sea.
15. A nobleman.
17. King of Crete.
19. The labyrinth was a famous one.
21. Husband of Helen.
22. Lives in fear.
23. He was persuasive.
24. Could be an honorable circumstance.
25. It burned to the ground.
26. Daughter of Minos.

Down

2. He flew too close to the sun.
3. A priest killed by a snake.
6. Working hard and steady.
8. Daedalus was accused of helping him.
11. A sacred image of Athena.
12. Son of Achilles.
13. Home of the labyrinth.
14. King of Ithaca.
16. King of Sicily.
18. Half man, half bull.
20. King of Troy.

NOTES

1. Michael Grant and John Hazel, *Gods and Mortals in Classical Mythology* (New York: Dorset Press, 1979), 262.

2. J. E. Zimmerman, *Dictionary of Classical Mythology* (New York: Harper and Row, 1964), 51.

3. Catherine B, Avery, ed., *The New Century Handbook of Greek Mythology and Legend* (New York: Meredith Corp., 1962), 200.

—FIVE LOVE STORIES—

Pyramus and Thisbe

THE PLAY

Cast of Characters
In Order of Appearance

Narrator
Pyramus, youth living in Babylon
Thisbe, the girl next door

Narrator: Have you ever wondered why mulberries are red? The change from white berries to red berries came about because of the love that two young neighbors had for each other. They lived in Babylon in what we would call a duplex or townhouse. Throughout their childhood they were playmates and as teenagers they found themselves in love. Their parents were much against a marriage, so they had to be content to talk to each other through a chink in the wall.

SCENE 1. A room with a wall from upstage center to downstage center.

Pyramus is on one side of wall and Thisbe on the other.

[curtain]

Pyramus: [he knocks gently on wall] Thisbe, can you hear me?

Thisbe: Yes, Pyramus, I can hear you.

Pyramus: If only our parents would let us mingle with one another. I could see no harm in our enjoying each other's company.

Thisbe: I want with all my heart to see you.

Pyramus: Perhaps if we explained to them that we would have a chaperon, they would be receptive to the idea.

Thisbe: My father refuses to let me have any friends much less a boy next door.

Pyramus: Do you have a trusted nurse that might arrange something for us?

Thisbe: Yes, I have a trusted nurse. My father trusts her and she is devoted to him.

Pyramus: Well, thank the wall that allows us to communicate with one another. Of course, if it were not for this wall, I could take you in my arms and kiss you.

Thisbe: But at least the wall lets us speak to one another. [kissing the wall and talking to it] Thank you wall. Thank you for taking this kiss to Pyramus.

Pyramus: Now wall, transport this kiss to Thisbe.

Thisbe: I received your kiss, dear Pyramus. Now you take another kiss of mine. I will smother you with kisses, my beloved. [kisses the wall many times]

Pyramus: Dear Thisbe, sweet dreams. I will talk to you in the morning.

Thisbe: Wait, Pyramus. Do not go yet. I cannot live like this. I wish to feel your strong arms around me. Please, let us find a way to be together.

Pyramus: We could steal away. Perhaps we can meet out in the country, beyond the city walls.

Thisbe: But how shall we do this?

Pyramus: Tomorrow, wait until after the sun sets. Then go out the gates just before they are closed for the night.

Thisbe: Yes, oh, yes, this is a marvelous idea. But where shall we meet?

Pyramus: At the tomb of Ninus. There is by the tomb, a tall mulberry tree full of snow white berries, and nearby a running creek.

Thisbe: I will be there. About three hours after the sun sets, when the moon is out, I will be at the tomb.

Pyramus: Wall, take my kisses to Thisbe. It will be the last time you have to transport my kisses as the next time I kiss Thisbe I will take her in my arms. I love you, Thisbe.

Thisbe: I love you. Sweet wall, take my kisses to Pyramus.

[curtain]

SCENE 2. By the tomb of Ninus, that next night.

Thisbe: [enters from left] Pyramus, are you here? Do you hear me? [to audience] He must not have arrived as yet. I'm really not afraid, I'll wait quietly for him. [growls from offstage] But what is it that I hear? The sounds seem to come from behind the mulberry tree. [louder sounds] Who is it? What do you want? Gods on Olympus, help me. It is a lioness, dripping with blood. I must get away. [Thisbe exits left quickly, dropping her cloak in front of the tomb of Ninus]

Narrator: Thisbe got away. However, the lioness took Thisbe's cloak in her mouth and shook it vigorously before dropping it and disappearing into the woods. Needless to say, this caused problems.

Pyramus: [enters from left] Thisbe, are you here? [sees the cloak] Apollo save me. It cannot be. But it must be. I allowed my own sweet loved one to come here alone. It is I who killed her. [picks up the cloak and kisses it over and over, while he walks over to the mulberry tree] Now I shall die, too. [he pulls his sword and sinks it into his breast]

Thisbe: [enters from left] Pyramus, have you come. I cannot seem to see. [she sneaks around, sees something on the ground, shudders, and then comes closer for a look] Pyramus, Pyramus, speak to me. [throws herself next to him and holds him in her arms kissing him] It is I, your Thisbe, your dearest. [he opens his eyes, sees her, and dies]

Thisbe: [picks up her cloak and holds it to herself] Your love for me has killed you. Death could be the only thing that could keep us apart. Not the wall. Not our parents. And I will not allow death to keep us apart.

Narrator: Thisbe plunged the same sword that killed her intended husband into her own heart. Ever since, the mulberry tree, drenched with blood of the two young lovers, blossoms forth with red berries.

[curtain]

Pygmalion and Galatea

THE PLAY

Cast of Characters
In Order of Appearance

Narrator
Pygmalion, youth living in Cyprus
Youth #1, friend of Pygmalion
Youth #2, friend of Pygmalion
Galatea, living sculpture

SCENE 1. Art studio of Pygmalion.

On stage are Pygmalion and two friends.

[curtain]

Pygmalion: No, I can't see wasting my time going to a party.

Youth #1:   You will become stale if you shut yourself up in this place.

Youth #2:   Just a night off once in awhile will help you relax and you will then work better. An artist deserves some time off.

Pygmalion: Look, I really can't see spending my time at a party when I could be working on my sculpture.

Youth #2:   Are you planning on abandoning society to live a life alone on the desert? Are you going to forever spend your holidays alone? If you shun all women now, how will you ever meet one with which to share happy times?

Pygmalion: And what about sad times? You make life with a woman sound like it is all happy times. I know better. Life has joys and sorrows and many of the sorrows are brought about by women.

Youth #1:   We are wasting our time. This fellow is impossible. Sorry you won't join us old buddy. We'll go and have a good time. [both exit left]

Pygmalion: [to statue] You will be the most beautiful statue in the world. You will have some of the grace, beauty, and charm of a rare goddess. I would never say or even hint that you would be as beautiful as a goddess because that would bring down the wrath of Aphrodite, whom we know to be the most beautiful. This island of Cyprus is a favored spot of hers because it was off these shores that she was born from the sea foam. The waves carried her here so she has a real love of our island. And she will watch my work, I know. [as he talks he works on his statue]

[dim lights for a few seconds]

Pygmalion: This statue does not look like a statue. No one would ever know that it is ivory and stone. When I look at this woman, I see the perfect woman, one with no deficiencies. I have made the perfect woman. Would that she be real and not of stone. [stands back and looks at her] My eyes feast on nothing but her. In fact, life is an empty dream without her. [knocking on door] Now who could that be? [opens door left]

Youth #1:   So you are finally finished. [stands back and looks at statue] You achieved what you started to do. Truly this is a masterpiece. One would think that this statue is real.

Pygmalion: [touching statue] Only that the ivory is cold to the touch but not to the eyes.

Youth #1:   You sound sad. Why so, when you have created this superb piece of art?

Pygmalion: Who cares for the art? My life is ruined. I love this cold image of a woman. I can think of nothing else but her; yet, she remains lifeless.

Youth #2:   You need to get out of here. We came by to see if you wished to join us in the festival for Aphrodite. The incense is burning, and the sacrifices are being made ready. Come join us in the festivities.

Pygmalion: It is useless to try to cheer me. However, I have nothing to lose by going to a festival for the beautiful goddess. Maybe I will join the other youths on the island who plead with Aphrodite to help them find a suitable mate, but I do not want a suitable mate. I want my statue.

Youth #2: Keep talking like that and you won't be around to even see your statue. Let's go.

[curtain]

Narrator: Many Cyprians were marching in the procession, bearing gifts to Aphrodite, some to placate her, some to beg her, and all to worship her. Pygmalion and his friends were

part of the procession to the temple. We find Pygmalion kneeling before the altar. [Pygmalion enters right and kneels sideways in front of curtain; spotlight on Pygmalion]

Pygmalion: [standing in front of curtain at stage left] Most special and beautiful goddess, Aphrodite, I do beseech you to bring my statue to life. This maiden made of ivory is everything to me. I love her. She is my own. [he bows his head and then raises it and looks across the stage] I do believe I see the flames of the altar fire burning brightly. Yes, three times I saw them burn up brightly. This is a good omen. Perhaps Aphrodite has answered me. [exits right]

[curtain]

SCENE 2. Pygmalion's art studio.

Pygmalion: [enters left and walks across stage to statue] I see a faint blush on your face. [he touches her arm] And is there a faint warmth to your flesh? [statue comes down from pedestal and Pygmalion and statue embrace] This is truly the doing of Aphrodite. Thank you dear goddess. [looking at the now alive statue] I will name you Galatea and we will marry.

Galatea: You are telling me that I am alive? Is this what being alive means? That I can talk and walk? [she takes a few steps back and forth swinging her skirt] How will I learn what life is all about?

Pygmalion: You will be my fair lady. There will be no problem. Just teaching you about life will be my greatest joy. I am sure that it was Aphrodite, the patroness of this island of Cyprus, who heard and answered my prayer. I will show her my gratitude by treating you well, but remembering always that it was Aphrodite that brought us together.

Galatea: [worriedly] You will tell me what to do? How to behave? How to speak properly?

Pygmalion: Never fear. I love you, Galatea.

Narrator: And so they lived happily, at least as far as we know. They had a son whom they named Paphos. That son gave his name to the favorite city of Cyprus.

[curtain]

Orpheus and Eurydice

THE PLAY

Cast of Characters
In Order of Appearance

Narrator
Orpheus, musician and poet
Rabbit #1
Rabbit #2
Eurydice, bride of Orpheus
Hermes, escort of the dead
Cerberus, three-headed dog
Hades, god of Underworld
Persephone, queen of Underworld

SCENE 1. A garden.

Narrator:	This is another story of two young lovers. No one could play or sing like Orpheus. People would stop whatever they were doing if they heard his music. Even wild beasts came out of their dens and the birds dropped from the sky to the closest tree if they heard him sing accompanied by his lyre.
[curtain]	
Orpheus:	It is spring. I love to be alive. Just a short time ago the lovely maiden Eurydice became my wife. My joy is complete. [he picks up his lyre which leans against a tree and begins to play; the tree bends and sways; two rabbits come from stage right; they dance to the music]
Rabbit #1:	Why are you so joyful, Orpheus? Your music is the best I have ever heard. Of course, I know that your mother, Calliope, was one of the Muses, and that you were born with talent, but still today you are even more magnificent than ever ...
Rabbit #2:	[interrupting] Yes, those here in Thrace fostered his talent. It isn't all heredity.

Rabbit #1:   Orpheus has no rival anywhere, except of course for the gods.

Orpheus: Let us not argue about my talent. Rather, let us rejoice in the happiness of the day for today the sweet Eurydice became my bride. In fact, here she comes now with her bridesmaids. [rabbits exit left]

Eurydice: [enters from upstage right with two bridesmaids] I heard you playing your lyre. When it comes to music, you have no peer on earth. I know that out lives together will be full of song, lighthearted and joyous.

Orpheus: [puts down lyre] Just seeing you puts music in my heart. My father, the prince, has had a great feast prepared and there will be music and dance. We must not keep the assembly waiting, so let us go at once to the party.

Eurydice: [to the bridesmaids] Come with us. You will have a wonderful time. [the group starts across stage] There will be many handsome princes present to shower you with attention. [stumbles and screams] Help me! A snake has just bitten my foot. I saw it too late to avoid it. [Eurydice slumps to the ground]

Orpheus: Gods help us. [kneels down and puts Eurydice in his arms] My wife is dead. No longer does she breathe. The day that started out so beautifully and offered a life of hope has ended in disaster. [Hermes enters right] Who are you? Why do you come in the midst of my sorrow?

Hermes: Of course you don't recognize me. I am Hermes. It is my job to escort those who recently died to the Underworld. I know that there is no such thing as sweet sorrow. Your heart is breaking and sadly enough I must now escort Eurydice to the land of the dead, where Hades, the king of darkness awaits her. [he takes the hand of Eurydice and she gets up and follows him offstage left]

Orpheus: [groans aloud] My life is ended. I am overcome with grief.

[curtain]

SCENE 2: A dark cave.

Orpheus and Cerberus are standing in front of the pulled curtain at right. Onstage are Hades, Persephone, and the Erinyes, who remain motionless until Orpheus enters stage.

[curtain]

Narrator: [standing in front of curtain at left] Orpheus was inconsolable. He wandered the earth looking for an occupation that would take his mind off his loss. He even accompanied Jason in his search for the Golden Fleece. He decided to do what few men had ever done. He would go to the Underworld and plead for his wife. Searching for the opening to the Underworld, he finally found it at the very end of the earth.

Orpheus: What need I do to get past you?

Cerberus: [growling] All spirits get past me, but none ever return. You are more than a spirit. You have flesh and sinew. You must not pass these gates.

Orpheus: I am determined. Now that I have found the entrance to the Underworld, I will not be deterred.

Cerberus: I can't imagine why you want to come here. What is that you are carrying?

Orpheus: This is a lyre. Listen while I play for you.

Cerberus: Don't bother. [but Orpheus strums his lyre and Cerberus starts swaying to the beat of the music]

[Orpheus backs onto stage as Cerberus exits; stage is dimly lit; a faint spotlight illuminates the throne of the king of the dead and his queen, Persephone; the Erinyes linger nearby]

Orpheus: [singing]

You gods who claim all for the dark and quiet world
You are the master who must be paid
When the bill must be paid we are yours forever
But my dear wife was plucked too soon.
I cannot bear it. Please lend her back to me.

[king of the dead and Queen Persephone get up and move closer to Orpheus in order to hear better; the Erinyes weep]

Hades: Are you weeping for Eurydice?

Orpheus: Yes, my bride was escorted here by Hermes on our wedding day. Since then I have wandered. My life without her has no meaning.

Hades: Your singing is beautiful and your song touching; even the Erinyes are weeping, which is way out of character for them.

Persephone: Please husband, relinquish Eurydice. Orpheus is miserable without her. His songs have deeply touched me.

Hades: Why, Persephone, I have never seen you show any emotion one way or the other. Always you are so cold, so forbidding, so unrelenting. And now you are begging me to send Eurydice with her husband. This singing really upset you.

Persephone: Look at the Erinyes. [Erinyes are weeping] They, too, feel the effects of the music.

Hades: [to Erinyes] Leave, I don't like all this crying. [Erinyes exit left center]

Persephone: But you had big tears yourself. You are not as coldhearted as I thought. Perhaps my mother could even begin to like you a bit.

Hades: [ignoring Persephone's remark] Spirit, come here. [enter spirit from right] Go and find Eurydice and bring her here immediately.

Persephone: The song was lovely.

Orpheus: Thank you.

Hades: There is one stipulation. You must walk out of here and never turn back to see your bride. She will follow you but if you turn back, she will lose her opportunity to leave and Hermes will be there to escort her back to me. So remember this. Do not look back. [looking out stage right] She is coming. Do not look at her.

Narrator: Orpheus couldn't contain himself. His emotions ran over and he gave a quick look back just before stepping to the outside world. These star-crossed lovers were not to see each other again until Orpheus himself died some years later.

[curtain]

Baucis and Philemon

THE PLAY

Cast of Characters
In Order of Appearance

Narrator
Zeus, king of the gods
Hermes, messenger of Zeus
Hera, queen of the gods
Baucis, peasant living in Phyrgia
Philemon, husband of Baucis

SCENE 1. Mount Olympus.

Narrator: This is the story of an elderly couple who loved and respected each other, who loved the simple life they led, and, when given the opportunity, asked for nothing more than to be able to continue with each other for eternity.

[curtain]

Zeus and Hermes are engaged in conversation.

Zeus: I feel the urge to get away from courtly life. If you want to know the truth, I'm fed up with Hera's insane jealousy. Why even the music of Apollo's lyre is getting to me. It is one problem after another.

Hermes: Agreed, agreed. You need to get away. I'm ready for a bit of fun. How about I go with you?

Zeus: Good. You know, I'm even tired of nectar and ambrosia. I'd like to have some plain ordinary food. Just the thought of it makes my mouth water.

Hermes: Where shall we go? What preparations shall we make? Have you any ideas?

Zeus: For one thing I do not want to ask Iris if we can use her rainbow. The last time I slid down her rainbow, she tried to be funny and pointed it far away from my destination.

Hermes: Let us go to Phrygia. It has beautiful countrysides. We can really relax there.

Zeus: Excellent idea, especially since I want to test hospitality in that area. It has been a long time since I have checked up on Phrygia. You would be surprised at how many folks forget the everyday manners of being polite to strangers.

Hermes: We will have plenty of opportunity to check on this. [Hera enters left and pauses to listen]

Zeus: Yes, I am tired, tired of all the quarreling among the gods. And as I say, I get very tired of Hera's jealousy.

Hera: So you're tired of my jealousy! Well, I am tired of your antics that make me jealous. Why the time I hired the monster with a hundred eyes to watch you, his hundred eyes weren't even enough. Your behavior is a royal disgrace.

Zeus: Chatter! Chatter! Here she goes. If you would attend to royal duties and stop trying to control my destiny, we could be happy.

Hermes: Father, put this kind of talk behind you. Let us be off to Phrygia.

Hera: You keep an eye on him, Hermes.

[curtain]

SCENE 2. Inside a simple cottage in the countryside of Phrygia.

An old man and woman are sitting quietly. The woman gets up when she hears a knock on the door.

Baucis: [opening the door] Come in out of the cold. You must be nearly frozen. [she beckons to the two forsaken looking characters] Sit here by the fire and warm your hands.

Zeus: We will just stand here by the open grate, lovely lady. It is very kind of you to invite us in.

Hermes: Yes, we have knocked on hundreds of doors and all of them have been shut in our faces. What are your names?

Baucis: My name is Baucis and my dear husband is Philemon. We are poor people but we are contented and happy. All our needs are met, so we have time for each other, and time to thank the gods who make all things possible.

Philemon: It is nice to have you visit. We have very few visitors nowadays. Rarely does anyone darken our door. [to Baucis] I'll go out and get a fresh cabbage while you tend to the hearth.

Baucis: [busy about the hearth] We shall have a small supper. I'll get down a piece of pork and put it into the kettle with the cabbage. [she cuts down a piece of pork that is hanging from the rafters] This will make a tasty dish. Although simple, it is one of our favorites. [puts pork on table]

Zeus: Whatever you serve will be a rare treat. There is nothing like home-cooked food.

Hermes: So true.

Baucis: Here comes Philemon with the cabbage. [takes cabbage from Philemon] Just excuse me for a moment while I stir this in with the pork. [works at table]

Philemon: Come and sit by the table and let me pour you some wine. [pours from the pitcher into the cups]

Zeus: It is indeed a pleasure to be here with you. It is so good not to hear constant complaints. You are indeed a gracious host and hostess.

Philemon: Our lives are quiet for we hardly know our neighbors. It is rare that anyone speaks to us. We have lived here in this small cottage all our married lives. We are happy. Let me pour you more wine.

Baucis: [looking into the pitcher] Why this pitcher is full of wine. One would think that we haven't had any at all. [she puts her hand to her head as does Philemon and they pray silently with bowed heads]

Philemon: We have made a mistake. We are indeed sorry that we offered you such poor refreshments. We should have served you goose.

Baucis: Yes, we do have a goose. We are sorry. We will catch it and cook it at once. [they hurry out right]

Zeus: Poor folks, they are now worried that they didn't treat us right but I believe they did. [Zeus gets up and looks out of window] They are chasing the goose. This is fun. Come see, Hermes.

Hermes: That goose is too smart for them. He waits in one corner and this just lets them narrowly miss him. I didn't want any goose anyway, did you Father?

Zeus: No, the cabbage and pork were delicious.

Hermes: Wait, they just caught him by the tail. No, he got away. [walks over to door] Baucis and Philemon, come on in the house. We don't want any goose. We really love the dinner you made us. It was fit for gods. You were good to us.

[Baucis and Philemon enter and stay close to hearth]

Zeus: I am Zeus and this is my son, Hermes. You have been host and hostess to gods. We appreciate all that you have done for us. All guests who seek shelter in a strange land are under my protection, so of course I am very interested. Your neighbors, and I mean all of your neighbors, refused us entrance into their homes. They are punished as of now. Come see for yourselves. [Zeus beckons to Baucis and Philemon to come to the door] See for yourselves. Nothing but water. The countryside has disappeared.

Baucis: [weeping] We are sorry for them.

Zeus: Stop your crying. Those people were not even good to you, but you are generous to be thinking about them. Come now, dry those tears.

[curtain]

SCENE 3. Outside a beautiful temple.

Zeus, Hermes, Baucis, and Philemon are looking at temple.

[curtain]

Baucis: Where is our home? Where are we?

Philemon: I think this used to be our home, but now there stands a great temple of the gods.

Zeus: You are right. This temple is what used to be your simple home. But what wish can I grant to you? I wish to repay you for the kindly maner in which you welcomed us into your home. Talk it over between yourselves.

[Baucis and Philemon put their heads together and whisper]

Philemon: We wish to remain here as caretakers of the temple and since we have spent our lives together we wish to remain with each other even in death.

Zeus: That sounds agreeable to me, what about you Hermes?

Hermes: It is a good and thoughtful wish. It should be granted.

Narrator: And so Baucis and Philemon lived out their lives in the temple taking good care of it and pleasing the gods. As their time on earth drew to a close they noticed that they grew leaves and a common bark encircled them. They had only time to say farewell to each other before they became trees with a common trunk. Baucis and Philemon are together for all time.

[curtain]

Ceyx and Alcyone

THE PLAY

Cast of Characters
In Order of Appearance

Ceyx, king of Thessaly
Alcyone, Ceyx's wife
Maid #1
Maid #2
Hera, queen of the gods
Iris, goddess of the rainbow
Hypnos, god of sleep
Morpheus, god of dreams

SCENE 1. A room in the palace of Ceyx.

[curtain]

Narrator: Ceyx, the king of Thessaly had a smile whose brilliance lit up the skies, but this seemed quite natural as his father was the morning star. His wife, Alcyone, was a very strong character who knew her own mind. This seemed natural as she was the daughter of Aeolus, king of the winds. As the scene opens we find the two young people talking seriously to one another.

Ceyx: Alcyone, my sweet love, I must leave for a few days or so. Please try not to be sad.

Alcyone: No, no, dear Ceyx, do not leave me. What are you thinking to even suggest that we be parted? We have never been without each other, not one single day. Why? Why?

Ceyx: For some days the affairs of state have been perplexing me. I must go and visit my oracle.

Alcyone: Your oracle? Your oracle? Why this will require many weeks and you will have to travel by sea. No, you cannot go.

Ceyx:	Really I have no choice. I must consult my oracle. It is only there that I will trust advice given to me.
Alcyone:	[flings herself on the bench, crying aloud] I more than anyone know the terror of the sea. Don't forget that I am the daughter of the king of the winds. My childhood was spent listening to and watching the winds. I know firsthand what faces men at sea.
Ceyx:	[sitting down beside her] Come now, dear Alcyone. Be strong and sensible. My need to visit my oracle by far outweighs the possible danger of traveling by ship. I will take an experienced crew. You have no need to worry.
Alcyone:	This is not true. You do not know the sea, the wind, the thunder, the lightning. I do. [gets up and walks toward center facing audience] I cannot permit it. I will die first. [turns to Ceyx] Please, take me with you. Then at least we will die together. I can be happy if I die with you, but do not leave me here alone.
Ceyx:	This is impossible. The gods would never permit me to take you on a dangerous trip. Yes, I admit now that it will be fraught with danger. But I can survive. Just the knowledge of your love will carry me through.
Alcyone:	If I truly had the power to foresee the future I would say that I will never see you again. My inner being tells me. I will go to the shore to see you off. Dear Ceyx, my heart is broken.
Narrator:	[standing in front of curtain] Less than twenty-four hours after sailing, a fierce storm broke out and Ceyx was lost at sea. The next scene opens several months later with Alcyone, not knowing of the misfortune, awaiting her husband's return.

[curtain]

SCENE 2. Alcyone's dressing room.

Alcyone is seated at her dressing table. Enter two maids.

[curtain]

Alcyone:	Please plait my hair. I want to be ready when Ceyx comes home.
Maid #1:	Have you heard from the king, your majesty?
Alcyone:	[worried expression] No, I have not, but I have faith that he will soon be home.
Maid #2:	[taking Alcyone's hair in her hands, she begins to make one long plait] I feel that he will be here as soon as you are finished weaving your new gown. The gown that you

made for the king is beautiful, and yours too, will be elegant. Even though you are keeping your mind and fingers busy with your weaving, I can tell that you are anxious, my lady.

Alcyone: Yes I am. But I pray everyday to Hera that she will assist Ceyx in his voyage.

Narrator: The goddess Hera is touched by the prayers of Alcyone. Here we listen in on Hera as she gives instructions to her messenger, Iris.

[Hera and Iris stand at stage left; spotlight is on them]

Hera: I am deeply touched by Alcyone. She prays daily for one who has long been dead.

Iris: So Ceyx did lose his life at sea.

Hera: Yes, many months ago.

Iris: But of course, she does not know that.

Hera: True! True! Iris, I want you to find Hypnos, the god of sleep. You know of course, it won't be an easy trip, for he lives behind the land of the Cimmerians and in utter darkness. I doubt if you can slide down your rainbow. Everything will be silent. You will not hear a sound.

Iris: That is no problem. I'll go as far as I can on my rainbow. After that I'll enlist the help of Hermes. If he won't go with me, he could lend me his winged sandals, although I dare say they will be much too large. I know exactly where Hypnos lives. His son, Morpheus, told me all about the place. The only sound comes from the gently flowing stream, Lethe, that flows nearby.

Hera: Don't drink from that stream or you'll forget why I sent you.

Iris: Come now, Hera, I am a goddess and I am not subject to such stresses. But why are you sending me?

Hera: Tell Hypnos that I want him to send Alcyone a dream in which she learns the truth about her beloved Ceyx.

Iris: Away I go.

[curtain]

SCENE 3. Home of Hypnos.

Enter Iris. Hypnos is asleep on a couch.

[curtain]

Iris:	[standing by the sleeping Hypnos] Come, Hypnos, wake up, wake up.
Hypnos:	What in thunder is happening? Who is trying to awaken me, the god of sleep?
Iris:	It is Iris. I have an important message from Hera.
Hypnos:	[sitting up and rubbing his eyes] Why couldn't Hera hold off until I awakened naturally? I hate to have my sleep disturbed.
Iris:	I don't want to hear about it. It is so frightfully dull here. Just awaken enough to hear this message.
Hypnos:	Yes, yes, what is it?
Iris:	Hera has been troubled lately about the prayers of a mortal named Alcyone, whose father is king of the winds. She is the wife of Ceyx who was drowned during a terrible storm.
Hypnos:	[sinking back in bed] Storms are not my department. Good night.
Iris:	Wake up, Hypnos. It doesn't pay to irk Hera. Listen to me.
Hypnos:	[sitting up] Get to the point.
Iris:	Hera wants you to send Alcyone a dream in which she hears the truth about her dead husband.
Hypnos:	Oh, so that is it. Be gone. I'll take care of it.
Iris:	I hope you will do so now.
Hypnos:	Yes, yes. I'll call my son Morpheus.
Iris:	I'm going to get out of here now before I give in to temptation and fall asleep. [exits right]
Hypnos:	Morpheus, wake up. [walks over to exit left and yells again] Morpheus, do you hear me? Wake up. [Morpheus, rubbing his eyes staggers in from left]

Morpheus: What are you shouting so about?

Hypnos: You are to go to Alcyone, queen of Thessaly, and let her know that her husband is dead. Do it now so I can go back to bed and get some sleep.

Morpheus: That's a long trip and I'm so tired.

Hypnos: Stop complaining. I'm in charge here. Go now.

Morpheus: Yes, Father. I will go on my noiseless wings. After entering her window, I'll stand by her bed, but I'll take on the form of her drowned husband Ceyx. I'll cover myself with seaweed and be cold, wet, and miserable. Go back to sleep.

[curtain]

Narrator: And so Morpheus, who was a magician when it came to changing into various forms, became Ceyx and stood by Alcyone's bed.

[curtain]

Morpheus: Poor wife, I am here. It is Ceyx. I cannot stay with you because I am dead. Yes, dear wife, you were right. The winds came up strong and I drowned the very first night I was at sea. [exits left]

Alcyone: [sits up] I saw him. I saw him right here standing by my bed. So terrible he looked. So pale. He is dead and soon I will die. How could I go on living when I know his body is floating somewhere at sea.

Narrator: At dawn Alcyone was at the waterfront. She watched as a body floated in on the waves. Recognizing her dead husband, she leaped into the water. Alcyone felt her body changing as she started to float over the waves. She had wings; her body was covered with feathers. The gods had changed Alcyone and her husband Ceyx into birds. Today we can spot them flying over the waves together in loving harmony. Once a year the sea is calm because Aeolus, Alcyone's father, guards the winds. During this time Ceyx and Alcyone brood over their nest of kingfishers that floats quietly on the calm waters.

[curtain]

General Activities

KEEPING A NOTEBOOK

Have the students keep a notebook. Each time they meet a new character, a monster, a significant place, or an important body of water, have them record it in the notebook. This could be done toward the end of each period, or at the beginning of each class period serving as a review of yesterday's material. It could be assigned as regular homework.

MAKING A BRAND NAME SCRAPBOOK

Have students go through magazines clipping any advertisements they can connect with mythology. The students can sit in groups or work by themselves. If students find ads that they already have, have students clip them out anyway and trade with other students, who also may have more than one of a kind. When they have about ten different ads it is time to start making the scrapbook, which can be added to as they learn more mythology. Have students paste the ad or picture on a plain piece of paper. Next to it, have the students write a short explanation of the myth and why the company chose the name for the product. Some brand names to look for: Mobil Oil, Olympia cameras, Ajax cleanser, Aurora tissues, Mercury cars, Argus cameras, Zenith televisions, Atlas tires, Venus pencils, White Owl cigars, Pandora sweaters, and F.T.D. florists. Some examples follow:

Goodyear

Hermes was the special messenger of Zeus, a magician, and a protector of travelers. He wore winged sandals and cap and was noted for his speed. Goodyear chose the winged sandals as their symbol to show that their Goodyear tires will get you to your destination swiftly and safely.

Whirlpool washer

Charybdis was a hideous monster, a whirlpool located off the coast of Sicily, who three times a day sucked in water and spit it out. Many times the whirlpool sucked up ships and crews along with the water. The Whirlpool washer will suck up dirt just as Charybdis sucked up ships.

Take it one step further and look for pictures, not necessarily ads. For example, a beautiful vegetable garden will show that Demeter has Persephone with her. A picture of many whitecapped waves shows that Poseidon is racing his horses again. Pictures offer endless possibilities. Paste the picture in the scrapbook and write a brief explanation.

STAR PROJECT

This project requires library research. It can be divided and parts given to committees or it can be assigned as an individual project. Give each student copies of star charts. Have them circle all those constellations that have mythological names, and find out why the constellation was so named. On plain paper they should draw a diagram of the constellation, putting a gold star in the proper star position. To the right of this, they should write a short account of the constellation. Two examples follow:

Big Bear and Little Bear

Zeus fell in love with a maiden named Callisto. Hera was so upset by this that she turned Callisto into a bear after her son was born. When the boy was grown, Hera fully intended him to shoot the bear while hunting without knowing he was shooting his mother. Zeus came to the rescue, snatching the bear and putting her in the sky among the stars. Later, her son was placed beside her. They became known as Big Bear and Little Bear. Hera was so incensed at this, she asked the god Poseidon not to let the bears descend into the sea. Thus, they never set below the horizon.

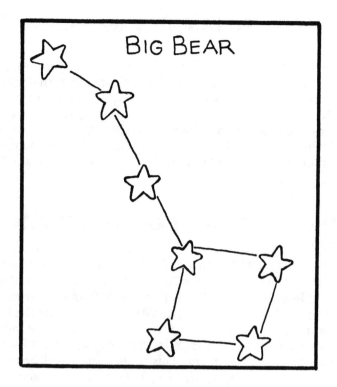

Draco

There is more than one dragon in mythology; hence, many stories are associated with Draco. He could be the monster that guarded the golden apples in the Garden of Hesperides or he could be the dragon that guarded the Golden Fleece.

EXTEMPORANEOUS SPEAKING

Go through magazines and cut out pictures of flowers, creeks, oceans, mountains, lightning, waterfalls, birds' nests, jewelry, cows, owls, vegetables, anything that can be connected with mythology. Paste these pictures on various color construction paper. On the back write numbers, starting with ones, that are visible from a distance. Using masking tape, stick all the pictures on the blackboard so the pictures cannot be seen and numbers are visible to the class. In a bowl or jar place corresponding numbers. Have a student pick a number from bowl, then match it with picture on the board. Student has one minute to make up a myth. Student can be judged on content, originality, and delivery.

MYTHO GAME – GENERAL INSTRUCTIONS

MYTHO is played like Bingo. Using the MYTHO card master (see next page), photocopy blank cards for each student in the class. Using red felt tip pens, have students write numbers of their choice (picking from 1-10 to put under the M, from 11-20 to put under the Y, from 21-30 to put under the T, from 31-40 to put under the H, and from 41-50 to put under the O) in the small squares in the upper left-hand corner of the large squares of the card. (It is a good idea to write on the blackboard the range of number choices for each letter.) Teachers should make up a large master sheet with 50 squares showing all the numbers. This master sheet will become the master answer sheet also. As random numbers are called (e.g., M-4, Y-23, etc.), the teachers ask a question from the list of 50 questions provided with each play. Students write the answers to the questions in the appropriate box on their cards next to the number, if they have that number. A completed column, row or diagonal is a MYTHO! The teacher can check the winner's card against the master sheet.

MYTHO GAME CARD

M	Y	T	H	O
		■		

PRODUCTION NOTES FOR PUPPET PLAYS

Have the following committees: music, sound effects, puppets, costumes, scenery, and production.

Music: Music can be played between acts and whenever the committee feels it would be appropriate. Have a committee of three students pick the proper music. They should put all the correct music on one tape, timing it so they know exactly when to turn the tape recorder on and off. Instead of dimmed lights to show passage of time, music could be played softly.

Sound effects: The sound effects committee goes through the play marking all places where sound effects are necessary. Some of the sounds can be found on commercial tapes, such as the roar of the ocean. Others they must make for themselves (they can probably find an uninhibited student who will cry, groan, and scream with relish).

Puppets: The majority of the class will be busy making the puppets. Assign each student a puppet. The student making the Cyclops should be reminded that the puppet will have a larger head than the other puppets. When making Demeter, have the student make two identical puppets, one dressed like an old lady and the second resplendent as a goddess.

Costumes: A committee can make these or each student can be assigned to make one costume. Or the person making the puppets can also make the outfit for that particular puppet. It is really a matter of the chemistry of the class.

Scenery: Three or four artists in the class should do the scenery. Butcher paper can be glued together to make the correct size backdrop. (See folding puppet theater section that follows.) The scenes are tacked to the wooden rods that are across the top-back of the theater. The scenes are hung in order, and after each scene the rod is lifted up and hung in the back position. (See diagrams of theater)

Production: The production committee is in charge of taping the show, collecting the props, making the programs, and any other jobs that are necessary, such as securing small chairs for the puppeteers. When making the master tape, the students do not have to memorize their parts but should be able to read them with expression and without hesitation. Appoint one student as director. The actors gather around one desk close to the tape recorder. They watch the director for cues, as do the students in charge of music and sound effects. Remove staples from the script and paste script pages to construction paper to avoid the noise of pages being turned.

The Performance. You will need three puppeteers, two scenery persons, one tape recorder person, and two costume people. These people sit behind the stage. A script is taped up inside the theater where the puppeteers can read it and one is taped up where the costume people can read it. The costume people hand the correct puppets to the puppeteers. All this takes coordination and practice. If everything is set up in the room the students can practice whenever they have free time.

Instructions for Making Hand Puppets

Materials

    small balloons
    papier-mâché
    Gesso
    various paints
    yarn or hair switches
    black or brown construction paper
    odd pieces of material
    needles and thread
    sandpaper

Papier-mâché

1. You can buy papier-mâché in a hobby shop and mix according to directions.

2. Tear up newspapers in small pieces. Make a thick paste out of flour and water. Mix paper and paste, squeezing it in and out of your hands.

3. Tear up bits of paper napkins and using glue, slowly add layer after layer.

Procedure

1. Blow up balloons to size head you wish.

2. Cover balloons with papier-mâché, leaving the tie end sticking out with enough space to put in your index finger.

3. Let dry probably two or three days depending on heat and humidity in the room. Turn every day. Sand with fine sandpaper to get rid of rough edges.

4. Paint with Gesso. This fills in crevices.

5. Paint with whatever paint you want as flesh color.

6. Paint on eyes, etc.

7. Fringe some construction paper and make eyebrows.

8. Clothes:

    1. Cut a piece of material 27 inches x 8 inches.

    2. Fold material lengthways.

    3. Cut out neck in middle of fold.

    4. Turn material so the nice part is inside. Sew up both seams leaving two inches at the top for arm holes.

Folding Puppet Theater

The following drawing is an isometric view of a folding puppet theater. This theater is convenient for the classroom because is lightweight (about thirty pounds), compact, and folds flat (64 inches x 52 inches x 3 inches) for storage. The material cost is modest and the construction is simple.

Set up, the theater is 64 inches high, 52 inches wide, and 32 inches deep. These dimensions have been chosen to permit three puppeteers to sit behind and below the stage on kindergarten stools.

Although the 1 inch x 1 inch finished pine or fir used for framing is lightweight, if the joints are notched, glued, and nailed, and the masonite is glued and nailed as shown, the structure, with

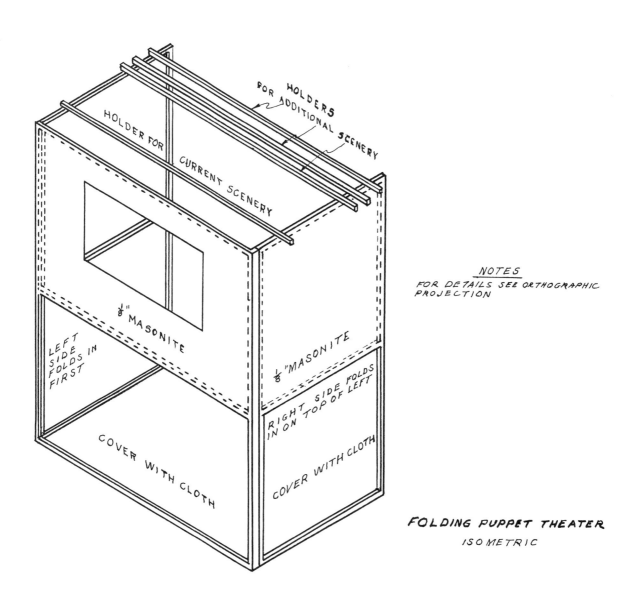

NOTES
FOR DETAILS SEE ORTHOGRAPHIC PROJECTION

FOLDING PUPPET THEATER
ISOMETRIC

reasonable care, will survive in a junior high classroom for a number of years. Please note that the notched 1 inch x 1 inch holders for additional scenery are essential to give rigidity to the open back of the theater.

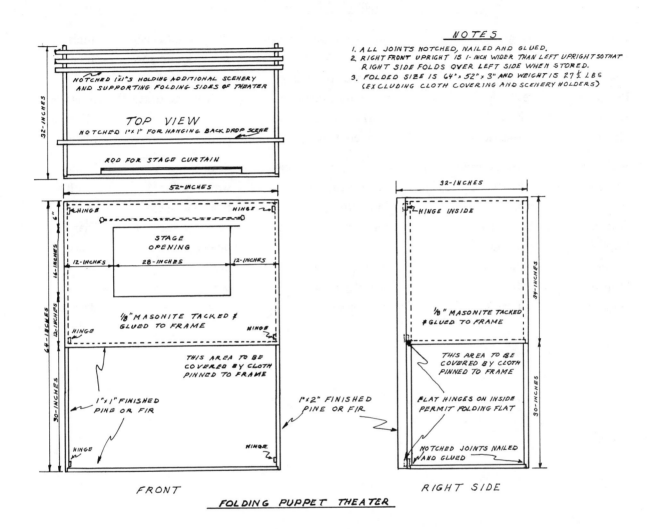

The orthographic projection gives the details of dimensions and material requirements. Please note the following:

1. Finished 1 inch x 1 inch stock is actually ¾ inch x ¾ inch.

2. Actual lengths and sizes of material are given. Material purchased must be according to standard lengths and sizes. There will be some waste in cutting to size.

3. The amount of cloth to cover the open bottom half of the theater is not given. If this curtaining material is pleated, the required yardage will be substantially greater than just the open areas indicated.

CHART OF THE GODS

The Olympian Gods

Greek	Position	Characteristic	Symbol	Roman
Zeus	king	strong, stupid, noisy	thunderbolt, eagle	Jupiter
Hera	queen	jealous, majestic	peacock and cow	Juno
Hades	underworld	terrible, forbidding	pronged fork	Pluto
Poseidon	sea	vindictive, dangerous	trident and horse	Neptune
Athena	wisdom	warlike, wise	owl	Minerva
Hermes	messenger	temperamental, shrewd	caduceus	Mercury
Aphrodite	love and beauty	irresponsible, loving	dove	Venus
Apollo	sun, music, medicine	benevolent, purifies	white mouse	Apollo
Ares	war	murderous, cowardly	boar and spear	Mars
Artemis	hunt, chase	loner, unapproachable	deer and she-bear	Diana
Hephaestus	fire and forge	kindly, peace-loving	quail	Vulcan
Hestia	home and hearth	quiet, unassuming	none	Vesta
Demeter	grain	sad, dependable	poppy	Ceres
Dionysus	wine	wild, mad	tiger	Bacchus

Answers

THE ODYSSEY

Discussion Questions

Act I

1. Ate the lotus and forgot everything.

2. Poseidon.

3. Poked his eye out.

4. Zeus.

5. Odysseus said that they needed supplies.

6. Hid himself under a ram to escape.

7. Persons be welcomed and given food before asking them their business.

8. Three Erinyes—Tisiphone, Alecto, and Megaera—all of whom live in the Underworld; born from the blood of Uranus, job is to relentlessly pursue the sinner. "These Erinyes are crones, with snakes for hair, dogs' heads, cold, black bodies, bats' wings and bloodshot eyes."[1]

Act II

1. So young.

2. Smoke.

3. Jealous.

4. Threw great boulders sinking ships and killing men.

5. Past the River Ocean.

6. His soul will wander aimlessly until he is buried properly.

7. Turned men into pigs.

8. Three Graces—Euphrosyne, Aglaia, and Thalia—presided over the social graces. They attended all banquets, receptions, and dances and were particularly interested in the arts.

Act III

1. A libation.

2. Sacrifice a barren heifer.

3. The oar he used to pull.

4. Not hurt the cattle of the sun god.

5. She died of sorrow.

6. Reaches out to her and weeps.

7. Because he has the reputation of being cunning, crafty, and sly.

8. Answers will vary.

Act IV

1. Keep himself from trying to join the singing Sirens.

2. So they wouldn't hear the singing Sirens.

3. Monsters; Scylla a six-headed monster who lived on a rock and Charybdis a whirlpool opposite her. In trying to avoid one, a ship stood a good chance of being caught by the other.

4. Eurylochus said he was made of iron.

5. Allowed Eurylochus to talk him into stopping at the island of the sun god.

6. Pleaded with Odysseus not to drop anchor at the land of Cyclopes; he complained and did not wish to explore Circe's island; he complained about not stopping at sun god's island.

7. Answers will vary.

8. Answers will vary.

Act V

1. Poseidon.

2. Hermes.

3. Calypso release Odysseus or incur the wrath of Zeus. Answers will vary.

4. Will take him by ship to his own land.

5. Asked him what he wanted before she served him refreshments.

6. Fond of Odysseus and unable to keep him with her.

7. Because this is a complete turn of events. Previously Calypso has been impervious to Odysseus's mental anguish.

8. List of the gods found in chart on page 234. When Dionysus invented wine he was made a god. To keep peace, Hestia allowed him to have her throne. Hades always lives in the Underworld.

Act VI

1. Daughter of King Alcinous.
2. Playing ball.
3. Answers will vary.
4. Does not want people to think he is her husband-to-be.
5. Early in act IV, Zeus said Phaeacians were kinsmen. You don't fight the kinsfolk of gods.
6. Kind and generous, she gives Odysseus food and clothing, she is intelligent, she understands that she should not be seen alone with Odysseus.
7. He serves wine and has a great feast prepared before he asks "Who are you?"
8. Answers will vary.

Test Yourself

1. Zeus
2. Odysseus
3. Polyphemus
4. Nobody
5. Calypso
6. Eurylochus
7. Hermes
8. Circe
9. Elpenor
10. Poseidon
11. River Ocean
12. Teiresias
13. libation
14. singing Sirens
15. Scylla
16. Charybdis
17. Nausicaa
18. Ithaca
19. Aeolus
20. Odysseus

Final Test

1. c
2. a
3. a
4. b
5. c
6. a
7. c
8. a
9. a
10. c
11. a
12. b
13. b
14. c
15. b
16. b
17. c
18. a
19. b
20. a

MYTHO Game

1.	pyre	18.	Laestrygonians	35.	Thrinacis
2.	Scherie	19.	Ithaca	36.	ten
3.	pinnacles	20.	Hermes	37.	they forgot everything
4.	Aeaea	21.	Eurylochus	38.	Ciconians
5.	Alcinous	22.	Ethiopia	39.	odyssey
6.	Aeolus	23.	Elpenor	40.	seven
7.	Hyperion	24.	Polyphemus	41.	wine
8.	moly	25.	Charybdis	42.	ram
9.	Olympus	26.	Circe	43.	smoke
10.	nectar	27.	Aeolia	44.	drink blood
11.	Ogygia	28.	Phaeacians	45.	wax
12.	Agamemnon	29.	Poseidon	46.	Hyperion
13.	Athena	30.	Arete	47.	Trojan
14.	seven	31.	Scylla	48.	Hermes
15.	Odysseus	32.	Teiresias	49.	Charybdis
16.	Nausicaa	33.	Zeus	50.	trident
17.	libation	34.	Poseidon		

THE GOLDEN FLEECE

Discussion Questions

Act I and Prologue

1. Half man and half horse.

2. His oracle.

3. Pelias was told by the oracle that a man wearing one sandal would kill him.

4. Because of his music.

5. Answers will vary.

6. Answers will vary.

7. Pelias made a promise and had no intention of keeping it.

8. Answers will vary.

Act II

1. Only women there.

2. Hypsipyle.

3. Winged female creature, foul odor.

4. Took his food.

5. Man the deck, everybody to his station, ready the dove, play the lyre.

6. Answers will vary.

7. Because he has the gift of prophecy.

8. Answers will vary.

Act III

1. Watching Zeus.

2. Fifty.

3. Master at witchcraft.

4. Try to get Aphrodite to have her son shoot an arrow at Medea.

5. Says "Hera must want something."

6. Answers will vary.

7. Ganymede yells that Eros has been cheating.

8. Cupid and Eros refer to the same god who was the youngest god and the son of Aphrodite. He is "generally shown as a pretty child, a little winged archer, capricious and mischievous, delighted in working magic by shooting invisible arrows at gods and men alike."[2] "Sometimes he is shown blindfolded to indicate that young people may fall in love blindly. We know him as Eros and Cupid. Both names left traces. Anything which arouses feeling of romantic love is said to be 'erotic' and 'cupidity' describes too much love of money and material things."[3] In some tales he is portrayed as a handsome young man, as in the case in a later play *Psyche*. In this play he is the mischievous child.

Act IV

1. Surrounds them in a rainy mist.

2. His courage.

3. Answers will vary.

4. Answers will vary.

5. Had them refresh themselves and have dinner before he asked them what they wanted.

6. More loyalty to Jason.

7. Jason felt that it was a reflection on his strength.

8. Jason and Odysseus: both of royal birth, both dealt with monsters, both showed courage, both helped by gods.

Act V

1. Even though they came to Colchis to take Aeetes's prized possession, they are treated royally.

2. King has no intention of keeping the promise.

3. Will become his wedded wife.

4. Will sing a special lullaby to put it to sleep.

5. Hypnotizes him.

6. Watches over him, even to sending sea nymphs to carry him through the straits where Scylla and Charybdis live.

7. No reason to suspect that King Aeetes was anything but honorable.

8. Asclepius, son of Apollo, was the god of medicine. At birth (his mother, Coronis, was a mortal, who died just before his birth) he was given to Chiron, the good Centaur to rear. From both his father and Chiron, he learned medicine and is considered the father of medicine. He succeeded too well and brought people back to life. This irritated Hades who complained to Zeus that Asclepius was ruining his business. Zeus promptly sent a thunderbolt to dispatch Asclepius. Apollo was really incensed that his son was treated so irreverently. However, he did not wish to take his father to task about this so he killed the Cyclops who made the thunderbolt. Asclepius, holding a serpent, was set among the stars, probably to appease Apollo. Serpents were special to medicine because serpents were known to shed their skins thus renewing themselves.[4] The caduceus, winged wand of Hermes, usually had two serpents twined around it, a symbol of the medical profession. Asclepius had many children among them Hygieia (health) and Panaceia (cure-all).

Act VI

1. Liked children, hoped to have a family, liked magic.

2. Traveled to dark side of the moon to see Hecate.

3. Rejuvenate him.

4. Aphrodite.

5. Promised to make Medea his wife, but now that he is home safely, he sees a better opportunity in a marriage to the king of Corinth's daughter.

6. Didn't know that Medea was a real witch. Medea got to know them by feigning interest and led them to believe that she would help them.

7. Did exactly what she said even though it was extremely distasteful to them.

8. Symplegades are clashing rocks at the mouth of the Black Sea. These treacherous rocks continually came at each other, making it almost impossible for a ship to pass safely.

   Scylla was a destructive sea nymph who was once a beautiful maiden much loved by Glaucus. Circe was a witch who loved Glaucus. When he did not return her favor, Circe changed Scylla into a six-headed monster resembling an octopus. Scylla spent her days grasping at sailors and eventually became a rock.

   Charybdis was a whirlpool who twice a day sucked up water and ships who happened by at the time.

   The singing Sirens were similar to Harpies but not evil smelling, nor did they have the ability to snatch their prey. Generally represented as birds with heads of women, they caught their prey by luring them with seductive voices and songs.

   Harpies were loathsome bird-like women, with huge wings and a terrible stench and claws that made it easy for them to snatch and hold their prey.

   Argus was a monster with one hundred eyes. Hera, being insanely jealous, hired him to watch over Zeus. Zeus had Hermes lull Argus's eyes to sleep and kill him. Hera then set his one hundred eyes in peacock feathers.

Test Yourself

1.	Phrixus	11.	Charybdis
2.	Chiron	12.	ambrosia
3.	Colchis	13.	Eros
4.	Orpheus	14.	Medea
5.	Calais	15.	Olympus
6.	Hypsipyle	16.	Nymphs
7.	Harpies	17.	Styx
8.	Amazons	18.	Zeus
9.	Scylla	19.	Hylas
10.	Iris	20.	Hera

Final Test

1.	c	6.	a	11.	a	16.	b
2.	c	7.	c	12.	b	17.	b
3.	c	8.	a	13.	a	18.	a
4.	b	9.	c	14.	c	19.	a
5.	a	10.	b	15.	a	20.	c

MYTHO Game

1.	Centaur	18.	Hypsipyle	35.	the nymphs
2.	Hercules	19.	Styx	36.	recalcitrant
3.	Jason	20.	Harpies	37.	quest
4.	Pelias	21.	Talus	38.	intrusion
5.	oracle	22.	Phineus	39.	prophecy
6.	Diomedes	23.	Iris	40.	dominate
7.	Aeson	24.	Amazons	41.	beckon
8.	Polymele	25.	Symplegades	42.	inspire
9.	Phrixus	26.	Colchis	43.	liberate
10.	Dardanelles	27.	Olympus	44.	episode
11.	Golden Fleece	28.	oars and sails	45.	attitude
12.	Zeus	29.	Medea	46.	exploit
13.	Orpheus	30.	Eros	47.	assault
14.	Zetes and Calais	31.	Ganymede	48.	vulnerable
15.	Hylas	32.	Apsyrtus	49.	invincible
16.	Aeetes	33.	Scylla	50.	wrath
17.	Lemnos	34.	Charybdis		

THE GREATEST ATHENIAN

Discussion Questions

Act I

1. Father was King Aegeus of Athens.

2. Wished to travel to Athens via land; grandfather thought he should take a ship across the Saronic Gulf.

3. Answers will vary.

4. Answers will vary.

5. Close one; went fishing together; Theseus felt free to disagree.

6. Answers will vary.

7. Answers will vary.

8. Listens carefully to his mother; disagrees politely with grandfather; he is his own self following his own lead.

Act II

1. Theseus wiped out vicious monsters.

2. Get Theseus out of the way so that her son might inherit the throne.

3. King was scared that Theseus would help the fifty sons of his half-brother.

4. Answers will vary.

5. Answers will vary.

6. Answers will vary but someone had to travel back to Troezen with the news.

7. Answers will vary.

8. Periphetes owned a huge club with which he killed passersby.
    Sinis would bend pine trees down until they reached earth. He would ask passersby to help him and then he would let go hurling the helper into the sky.
    Sciron was a bandit who sat on high cliff. He demanded that passersby would wash his feet. When they stooped over he kicked them off the precipice into the sea where giant turtles waited to devour them.
    Cerycon would challenge folks to wrestle and then crush them to death in his embrace.
    Procrustus offered a night's lodging to travelers and put short men in a large bed and tall men in a short bed and either stretched them to fit or cut their legs off to fit.

Act III

1. To find a way out of the labyrinth for Theseus.

2. 1, 5, 7, 2, 8, 6, 3, 4.

3. Answers will vary.

4. Presented a problem of loyalty to her father.

5. Answers will vary.

6. Answers will vary.

7. Answers will vary.

8. Both Ariadne and Medea were daughters of kings, both fell in love with heroes, both sacrificed loyalty to their fathers in order to help their beloveds, both left home with heroes, both in a sense were abandoned by heroes.

Act IV

1. Government of the people (democratic).

2. Because the souls of the dead wander until bodies are given proper burial.

3. Courageous and just man and cannot watch others commit an injustice on a fellow human being.

4. Answers will vary.

5. Democratic.

6. Visitor feasts and rests before stating his business.

7. Answers will vary.

8. Democratic is more than one party, all voices can be heard, equality of rights, state exists for the people.
    Totalitarian is one political party, suppression of opposition, people exist for the state.

Act V

1. Wanted to see for himself if Theseus was as great a hero as proclaimed.

2. Liked the up-front honesty of Pirithous.

3. Answers will vary.

4. Answers will vary.

5. Answers will vary.

6. Call truces to bury the dead, use bows and arrows, women fought in hand-to-hand combat.

7. Because the Amazons were such sharpshooters they could kill while shooting from shore.

8. Legendary race of war-loving women, who lived on the south coast of the Euxine Sea in a country that excluded men. Hercules, as one of his labors, had to secure the girdle of Amazon Queen Hyppolita.

Act VI

1. Answers will vary.

2. The Underworld.

3. Probably, because of the oath Theseus accompanied Pirithous to the Underworld.

4. Tried to stead Theseus's cattle, visit the Amazons, tried to kidnap Persephone.

5. Answers will vary.

6. Answers will vary.

7. Answers will vary.

8. Answers will vary.

9. Answers will vary.

Test Yourself

1. Scyros
2. Black Sea (Euxine Sea)
3. Pirithous
4. Daedalus
5. Ariadne
6. Minotaur
7. Androgeus
8. Theseus
9. Saronic
10. Medea
11. Hercules
12. King Pittheus
13. Aethra
14. Aegeus
15. Medus
16. Crete
17. Amazons
18. Antiope
19. Phaedra
20. Hippolytos

Final Test

1. a
2. c
3. c
4. a
5. b
6. a
7. c
8. a
9. b
10. b
11. a
12. c
13. c
14. c
15. a
16. b
17. a
18. b
19. b
20. a

PERSEUS

Discussion Questions

Act I

1. Brother.

2. Dictys gave Danaë water, fruit, and bread.

3. Polydectes was annoyed when his brother came to see him without an invitation.

4. Probably would have been brought up in King Acrisius's court, but answers could vary.

5. Would be brought up in the court of either Acrisius or Polydectes.

6. Answers will vary.

7. Answers will vary.

8. Gray Sisters are portrayed as old hags, with grey hair and skin with many folds. They share one eye and one tooth among them. Some stories have them living at the foot of Mount Atlas, others north of the Cimmerians, and still another account north of the Hyperboreans. They are sisters to the Gorgons and are famous for their part in the story of Perseus.

   Hyperboreans, inhabitants of a mythical nation reportedly situated behind the North Wind, although sometimes mentioned to the east or northwest of Greece. Supposedly they were happy people untouched by human illness.

   Gorgons were three frightening sisters, who lived in the far west near the River Ocean. All sisters were hideous but one look at Medusa was enough to frighten a man into stone. Medusa had snakes for hair, a protruding tongue, warts, a beard, and a terrible grin.

Act II, Scenes 1 and 2

1. Hippodamia.

2. Answers will vary.

3. That he is a silly youth.

4. Winged sandals, magic wallet, and helmet of invisibleness.

5. Lonely in a strange city.

6. Answers will vary.

7. Probably youth and impulsiveness but answers could vary.

8. Medusa violated one of Athena's temples, outraging the goddess. She turned Medusa from a beautiful maiden into a winged monster so frightful in looks that she literally scared people to death. She had snakes for hair, two frightful teeth, and a protruding tongue.

Act III, Scenes 3 and 4

1. Far north of the Cimmerians.

2. They fought over one eye.

3. Pemphredo.

4. Answers will vary. A good example in parking in handicapped parking when they are able-bodied.

5. He would have been turned to stone.

6. Answers will vary.

7. Perseus wore the helmet of invisibleness.

8. Both Perseus and Theseus were brought up in kingdoms other than their fathers', both were strong and courageous, both fell in love with maidens they met on a journey, both took their widowed mothers to live with them.

Act IV

1. Being sacrificed to appease the sea goddesses who were offended by her mother's claims of beauty.

2. Because Cepheus overheard Perseus tell Andromeda he wanted her to be his wife and Cepheus saw a way to save her from the serpent.

3. Her great beauty.

4. Answers will vary.

5. Answers will vary.

6. Answers will vary.

7. Both were brought up by someone other than parents.

8. Answers will vary.

Test Yourself

1. Delphi
2. shield
3. Gray Sisters
4. Medusa
5. Hippodameia
6. Hermes
7. Stygian
8. Polydectes
9. Danaë
10. oracle
11. Acrisius
12. Seriphos
13. Zeus
14. Pegasus
15. Cassiopoeia
16. Cepheus
17. Phineus
18. Hyperboreans
19. Cimmerians
20. invisible helmet

Final Test

1. b
2. a
3. a
4. c
5. b
6. c
7. a
8. c
9. a
10. c
11. a
12. b
13. a
14. c
15. b
16. b
17. a
18. c
19. b
20. a

MYTHO Game

(The *Greatest Athenian* and *Perseus* combined)

1. Aethra
2. Daedalus
3. Pirithous
4. Antiope
5. Phaedra
6. King Aegeus
7. Troezen
8. Minos
9. Medus
10. sixteen
11. sandal and sword
12. Saronic
13. cousin
14. Aegeus
15. fifty
16. poison
17. avenge death of his son
18. Minotaur
19. maze
20. Crete
21. white
22. totalitarian
23. thread
24. Daedalus

25. Naxos
26. Gray Sisters
27. Acrisius
28. Polydectes
29. snakes
30. Dictys
31. Hermes
32. Athena
33. Stygian Nymphs
34. Cimmerians
35. Hyperboreans
36. River Ocean
37. vanity
38. King Cepheus
39. one year
40. Medusa's head
41. discus
42. Phaedra
43. Hippolytos
44. soul wanders
45. Black Sea
46. woman
47. Ares
48. Athenians
49. arrow
50. Hercules

PERSEPHONE

Discussion Questions

1. Sea nymphs.

2. Answers will vary.

3. Ask Helios.

4. Answers will vary.

5. A cloudy day, because it is no fun racing a chariot through clouds.

6. Answers will vary.

7. Answers will vary.

8. Hecate is one of the original Titans and the only one to keep her powers after Zeus took control.[5] Zeus allowed her to keep the power of giving or withholding gifts to mortals. She was the goddess of the dark side of the moon, those black nights when there is no moonlight. She is often called the goddess of the crossways—where three roads meet which in ancient times was considered to be an evil place.[6] Some mythologists have Hecate with three heads—that of a lion, dog, and horse—and others depict her as an old crone. After helping locate Persephone she spent most of her time in Hades where she and Persephone became close.

Test Yourself

1. Persephone
2. Zeus
3. Hermes
4. Hecate
5. Metaneira
6. Celeus
7. Hades
8. Demeter
9. sun
10. nymphs

Final Test

1.	c	11.	b
2.	a	12.	a
3.	a	13.	c
4.	c	14.	a
5.	c	15.	c
6.	a	16.	a
7.	b	17.	b
8.	a	18.	c
9.	c	19.	c
10.	a	20.	a

PSYCHE

Discussion Questions

Act I

1. Her beauty is such that people stop to gaze at her and worship her.

2. Because he knows that Aphrodite will be angry.

3. 6, 7, 5, 4, 3, 8, 2, 1.

4. Answers will vary.

5. Jealousy, envy.

6. Answers will vary.

7. Answers will vary.

8. Before earth, sea, and sky were created, only one thing existed, a shapeless mass called Chaos. This Chaos held the seeds of all things to come. Earth and heaven sprang from Chaos and were suitably named Gaea and Uranus. They in turn were the parents of Cronus and Rhea who in their turn become the parents of Zeus and Hera. Cronus and Rhea were Titans. Zeus rose up against his father and after a bitter struggle became lord of the universe.

Act II

1 . Kindly and firmly. She said that she could not help because gods stuck together.

2. Eros.

3. Answers will vary.

4. If she jumped off tower she would have been dead and unable to return from the Underworld.

5. Go to a dark cave, take two coins, take two pieces of hard bread, do not speak to anyone, do not open the box.

6. Answers will vary.

7. Curiosity.

8. Answers will vary.

Test Yourself

1. Apollo's oracle
2. precipice
3. Zephyr
4. Eros
5. monster
6. magic carpet
7. question
8. oil
9. love
10. temple
11. Demeter
12. Hera
13. Custom
14. servant
15. chicanery
16. ants
17. Sorrow, Anxiety
18. thicket
19. Persephone
20. curiosity

Final Test

1. c
2. a
3. a
4. c
5. b
6. c
7. b
8. c
9. a
10. a
11. b
12. a
13. c
14. a
15. b
16. b
17. b
18. c
19. a
20. c

MYTHO Game

(Persephone and Psyche combined)

1. Persephone
2. Goddess of grain
3. Hades
4. Hecate
5. Metaneira
6. barley water
7. Celeus
8. Zeus
9. chariot
10. nymphs
11. Narcissus
12. sun
13. far west
14. Sicily
15. Demophoön
16. sun
17. Hermes
18. pomegranate
19. winter
20. The Fates
21. Olympus
22. sea nymphs
23. gems
24. to be miserable
25. precipice
26. Aphrodite
27. Custom
28. ants
29. oil
30. thickets
31. Zephyr
32. oracle
33. Eros
34. monster
35. love
36. sea
37. chicanery
38. Persephone
39. Curiosity
40. eagle
41. Miletus
42. mischief
43. two
44. jealousy
45. Demeter
46. Sorrow and Anxiety
47. temple
48. see husband
49. locked up
50. Hera and Zeus

DAEDALUS

Discussion Questions

Act I

1. Daedalus is the architect.

2. Crete and Sicily.

3. Answers will vary.

4. Answers will vary

5. Answers will vary.

6. Because he didn't sacrifice the Minotaur.

7. Making the wings, flying out of labyrinth.

8. Daedalus literally means the "cunning worker." He was skilled in the mechanical arts, the patron of artists' and craftsmen's guilds. He was the grandson of Erechtheus, who invented axes, awls, bevels, and the like. He was envious of his nephew Perdix, also an inventor, whom he tried to kill.[7]

Act II

1. 6, 5, 8, 2, 1, 3, 4, 7.

2. Answers will vary.

3. He yells, gives impatient orders.

4. The labyrinth.

5. The oracle told him.

6. Because Minos knows Daedalus cannot resist a challenge.

7. He invented when the spirit moved him.

8. Answers will vary.

Test Yourself

1. Labyrinth
2. Daedalus
3. Icarus
4. ant
5. King Minos
6. Theseus
7. Odysseus
8. wax and feathers
9. Sicily
10. Poseidon

Final Test

1. c
2. a
3. c
4. a
5. b
6. b
7. b
8. a
9. a
10. a
11. b
12. b
13. c
14. c
15. a
16. c
17. a
18. b
19. a
20. a

THE WOODEN HORSE

Discussion Questions

1. Build a wooden horse and hide in it.

2. Taking the Palladium from the Trojans.

3. Answers will vary.

4. 6, 1, 5, 2, 8, 3, 7, 4.

5. Answers will vary.

6. Answers will vary.

7. Answers will vary.

8. Epeius was middle-aged, a master craftsman, physically weak, not too handsome, a coward.
   Neoptolemus was young, not good with a hammer, very strong, good looking, very brave.

Test Yourself

1.	Palladium	6.	Priam
2.	Diomedes	7.	Laocoön
3.	Neoptolemus	8.	Cassandra
4.	Trojans	9.	Sinon
5.	Epeius	10.	Menelaus

Final Test

1.	a	11.	b
2.	c	12.	c
3.	c	13.	c
4.	a	14.	b
5.	a	15.	b
6.	b	16.	a
7.	a	17.	c
8.	b	18.	c
9.	b	19.	a
10.	a	20.	b

MYTHO Game

(*Daedalus* and *The Wooden Horse* combined)

1. Minos
2. Daedalus
3. Ariadne
4. treason
5. Poseidon
6. half man and half bull
7. Icarus
8. Sicily
9. an ant
10. wax
11. Neoptolemus
12. Palladium
13. Trojans
14. over nine years
15. Odysseus
16. Epeius
17. master craftsman
18. eighteen
19. Epeius
20. Epeius
21. Odysseus
22. Sinon
23. heel
24. Priam
25. Odysseus and Diomedes
26. Cassandra
27. Laocoön
28. serpent
29. Aphrodite
30. fire
31. Neoptolemus
32. Daedalus
33. sacrifice him
34. his heart
35. Athenians
36. arrow
37. sacrifice to Minotaur
38. air
39. sea
40. selfishness
41. oracle
42. Sicily
43. in battle
44. Cocalus
45. a nobleman
46. Mediterranean
47. Italy
48. Greece
49. Greece
50. Athens

CROSSWORD PUZZLES

The Odyssey

The Golden Fleece

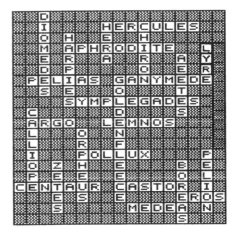

Greatest Athenian

Perseus

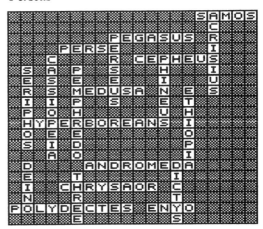

Persephone and Psyche

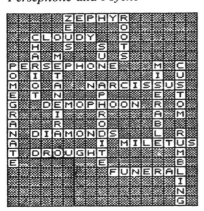

Daedalus and The Wooden Horse

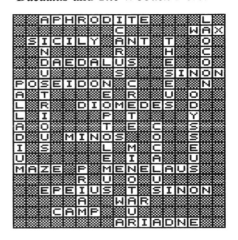

NOTES

1. Robert Graves, *The Greek Myths* (New York: Viking-Penguin, 1960), 1:122.

2. H. J. Rose, *A Handbook of Greek Mythology* (New York: E. P. Dutton, 1959), 123.

3. Isaac Asimov, *Words from the Myths* (Boston: Houghton-Mifflin, 1969), 60.

4. Michael Grant and John Hazel, *Gods and Mortals in Classical Mythology* (New York: Dorset Press, 1979), 56.

5. Thomas Bulfinch, *Bulfinch's Mythology* (New York: Avenal Books, 1979), 911.

6. Graves, 121.

7. Bulfinch, 898.

Glossary

Achilles (uh kill' eez). Greek hero in Trojan War.

Aeaea (ay ay' a). Island where Circe lived; Odysseus and Jason visited here.

Aeetes (ay et' es). King of Colchis; he had the Golden Fleece.

Aegeus (ay' gee us). Father of Theseus; king of Athens.

Aeneas (ay knee' us). Trojan warrior.

Aeolia (ay' o lee a). Home of Aeolus; Odysseus stayed here a month.

Aeolus (ay' o lus). Keeper of the winds; gave Odysseus a bag of winds.

Aeson (ay' son). Father of Jason; he entrusted Chiron with his son's education.

Aethra (ay' thra). Mother of Theseus.

Agamemnon (ag a mem' non). Brother of Menelaus and Greek warrior.

Alcestis (al ses' tis). Daughter of Pelias.

Alcinous (al sin' o us). King of the Phaeacians; he helped Odysseus reach Ithaca.

Alcyone (al sigh' o knee). Wife of Ceyx; daughter of King Aeolus.

Amazons (am' a zons). Warrior women; Theseus married one of them.

Andromeda (an drom' uh da). Daughter of Cepheus; married Perseus.

Antenor (an tee' nor). Trojan warrior.

Antiope (an tee' o pee). Queen of Amazons; married Theseus.

Aphrodite (af row dye' tee). Goddess of love and beauty.

Apollo (a poll' o). God of medicine, sun, and music.

Apsyrtus (ap sir' tus). Brother of Medea.

Ares (air' ees). God of war.

Arete (ah ree' tay). King Alcinous's wife.

Ariadne (air ee add' nee). Daughter of King Minos; she helped Theseus escape from labyrinth.

Artemis (are tum' us). Goddess of hunt and moon.

Asclepius (as klep' e us). God of healing; son of Apollo.

Athena (uh thee' na). Goddess of wisdom; daughter of Zeus.

Athenian (uh thee' ni an). Citizen of Athens.

Athens (ath' enz). Home of Theseus.

Babylon (bab' uh lon). City in Middle East where Thisbe and Pyramus lived.

Baucis (baa' cis). Wife of Philemon; showed hospitality to Zeus.

Calais (cal lay' is). Son of the North Wind.

Calliope (ca lee' uh pee). A muse; mother of Orpheus.

Calypso (ca lip' so). An enchantress; she held Odysseus captive seven years.

Cassandra (kay san' dra). Daughter of Priam of Troy. No one ever believed her.

Cassiopeia (cas ee o pee' ya). Wife of Cepheus; mother of Andromeda.

Cepheus (see' phoos). King of Ethiopia; father of Andromeda.

Cerberus (sur' ber us). Three-headed dog; guarded the gates of the Underworld.

Cerycon (sir sigh on). Crushed people while wrestling with them.

Ceyx (see' iks). King of Thessaly, husband of Alcyone.

Charon (share' on). He ferried souls of the dead across the river.

Charybdis (ka rib' dis). A whirlpool that sucked up ships.

Chiron (cheer' on). Wise and good centaur; he brought up Jason and Asclepius.

Cimmerians (see mee' ree uns). People who lived in a dark miserable place. No one ever sees them.

Circe (sur' se). One of two real witches in mythology; she turned Odysseus's men to pigs.

Corinth (cor' inth). Jason settled here.

Cyclopes (sigh clo' peez). One-eyed giants; they were Titans.

Cyprians (sip' ri an). People who live on Cyprus.

Daedalus (dead' uh lus). Architect of labyrinth; an inventive genius.

Danaë (dan' nigh). Daughter of King Acrisius of Argolis; mother of Perseus.

Deiphobus (dee if' o bus). Trojan warrior.

Deino (day' ee no). One of the Gray Sisters.

Demeter (duh mee' ter). Goddess of grain; mother of Persephone.

Demophoön (de' mo foon). Baby son of Metaneira.

Dictys (dick' tees). Fisherman; brother of Polydectes.

Diomedes (die o mee' des). Greek hero in the Trojan War; also given name of Jason.

Dionysus (die o nee' shus). God of wine.

Elpenor (el pee' nor). Young crewman of Odysseus; he fell off roof.

Elysian Fields (ee li' shee un). The virtuous went here after death.

Enyo (een' yo). One of the Gray Sisters.

Epeius (ep pee' us). He built wooden horse; born a coward.

Erinyes (ur rin' ne eez). Avenged wrongdoing; relentlessly pursued evildoers.

Eros (air' ros). Son of Aphrodite.

Ethiopia (e thee o' pia). Believed to be an area near Joppa, or south of Egypt; gods loved to go here.

Eurydice (u rid' uh see). Wife of Orpheus; bitten by a snake on wedding day.

Eurylochus (u ril' o kus). Crewman of noble birth; big complainer.

Fates (fatz). They decide a man's destiny.

Galatea (gal a tea' a). Name given to statue by Pygmalion.

Ganymede (gan i meed'). Olympian cupbearer.

Gorgons (gor' gons). Three ugly sisters with snakes for hair.

Graces (graces). Three sisters who presided over banquets, dances, and receptions.

Hades (hay' dees). King of the Underworld.

Harpies (har' peas). Foul-smelling, bird-like women.

Hecate (heck' a tee). Goddess of the dark side of the moon.

Helios (he' lee os). God of the sun; told Demeter the whereabouts of Persephone.

Hephaestus (hay fes' tus). God of fire and forge; husband of Aphrodite.

Hera (her' a). Queen of the gods; wife of Zeus.

Hercules (her cu' lees). Strong hero; cousin of Theseus.

Hermes (her' mees). Messenger of Zeus; escorts the dead to the Underworld.

Hestia (Hes' tee a). Goddess of home and hearth.

Hippodameia (hip pod i my' a). Fiancée of King Polydectes; wished to be given horses as engagement presents.

Hylas (hy' las). Armor-bearer of Hercules.

Hyperboreans (high per bo' ree ans). Happy people who lived beyond the North Wind.

Hyperion (high pier' i on). Sun god.

Hypnos (hip' nos). God of sleep.

Hippolytos (hip poll' it tus). Son of Antiope and Theseus.

Hypsipyle (hip sip' uh lee). Leader of women on Lemnos.

Icarus (ick' uh rus). Son of Daedalus; flew too close to sun.

Iris (i' ris). Goddess of the rainbow; messenger of Hera.

Ithaca (ith' a ka). Island off the west coast of Greece.

Jason (ja' son). Leader of Argonauts; he jilted Medea.

Labyrinth (lay' baa rinth). Maze built by Daedalus.

Laestrygonia (les trig o' knee a). Home of gigantic men and women.

Laocoön (lay oak' o foon). Trojan priest crushed to death by a serpent.

Lemnos (lem'nos). Island where fierce independent women lived.

Libation (li bay' shun). Liquid offering to the gods.

Lyre (lie' er). Musical instrument made by Apollo.

Medea (ma dee' a). One of two witches in mythology.

Medus (me' dos). Son of Medea.

Menelaus (men uh lay' as). Husband of Helen; Greek warrior in the Trojan War.

Metaneira (met a nigh' ra). Befriended Demeter and incurred her wrath.

Minos (my' nos). King of Crete; father of Ariadne and Phaedra.

Minotaur (min' uh tor). Half man and half bull.

Moly (mole' ee). Herb that makes one immune to witches' spell.

Morpheus (more' fuss). God of dreams; son of Hypnos.

Muses (muse' es). Nine sisters; goddesses of the fine arts and humanities.

Nausicaa (no sik kay' a). Daughter of King Alcinous.

Nectar (neck'tar). Drink of the gods.

Neoptolemus (knee op tol' uh mus). Son of Achilles; brave warrior in the Trojan War.

Ninus (nigh' us). Tomb where Thisbe and Pyramus were to meet.

Nymphs (nimfs). Minor goddesses; usually portrayed as young maidens.

Odysseus (o dis' oos). King of Ithaca; Greek hero who took ten years to return from the Trojan War.

Ogygia (o gi' gee ah). Island on which Calypso lived.

Olympus (o lim' pus). Mountain in Greece where gods lived.

Oracle (or' a cul). Priest from whom ancient Greeks sought answers.

Orpheus (or' fus). Musician and poet; husband of Eurydice.

Paphos (pa' fos). Son of Pygmalion and Galatea; name of city in Cyprus.

Pegasus (peg' a sus). Horse born of Medusa's blood.

Pelias (pee' lee as). He sent Jason in search of the Golden Fleece.

Pelopea (pee low pay' a). Daughter of Pelias.

Pemphredo (pem fred' do). One of the Gray Sisters.

Persephone (per sef' o nee). Daughter of Demeter; queen of the Underworld.

Perseus (per' sus). Son of Danaë.

Phaecians (fee a' shanz). People who lived in Scherie.

Phaedra (fee' dra). Another daughter of Minos.

Philemon (fi lay' mon). Husband of Baucis; showed hospitality to Zeus.

Phineus (fie' nus). Man bothered by Harpies.

Phrixus (frik' sus). He gave the Golden Fleece to Aeetes.

Phrygia (frig' eye a). Area in western Asia Minor; south of Black Sea.

Pinnacles (pin' uh cals). High points.

Pirithous (pie rith' o us). Friend of Theseus.

Pittheus (pitt' thoos). King of Troezen; grandfather of Theseus.

Polydectes (poly deck' tes). King of Seriphos; brother of Dictys.

Polymede (pol i mee' de). Mother of Jason.

Polyphemus (poly fee' mus). One-eyed giant; a Cyclops.

Poseidon (poh sigh' don). God of the sea; Earthshaker.

Priam (pry' um). King of Troy; father of Cassandra.

Procrustus (pro crust' tus). Bandit who either stretched people or cut their legs off in order that they fit a bed.

Psyche (sigh' key). Daughter of king of Miletus; married Eros.

Pygmalion (pig may' lee un). Sculptor in Crete; created the statue Galatea.

Pyramus (pier' a mus). Young man of Babylon; in love with Thisbe.

Pyre (pie' r). Large fire for burning corpses.

Scherie (ski' ree). Homeland of the Phaeacians.

Sciron (sigh' ron). Bandit who pushed people off cliffs.

Scylla (sil' a). Creature with twelve feet, six necks, and six heads.

Sicily (sis' uh lee). Island off coast of Italy.

Sinon (sigh' nun). Cousin of Odysseus; left as a decoy in Troy.

Sinus (sigh' nis). Thug who bent people as if they were trees.

Stygian nymphs (stig' ee un). They gave Persus the sandals, wallet, and helmet.

Styx (stiks). River in the Underworld.

Symplegades (sim pleg' a dees). Clashing rocks.

Talus (ta' lus). Last man of the Bronze Age.

Teiresias (tie ray' see us). Blind prophet in Hades.

Tenedos (ten' e dos). Island off coast of Troy.

Thessaly (thes' a lee). Area in Greece.

Thisbe (this' be). Young maiden of Babylon; in love with Pyramus.

Thrace (thras). Area north of Aegean Sea.

Thrinacis (thri nay' shuz). Hyperion pastured his cattle here.

Trojans (tro' jans). Citizens of Troy.

Zephyr (sef' er). West Wind.

Zetes (ze' tez). Son of the North Wind.

Zeus (zoos). Father of gods; Cloudgatherer.

Bibliography

Asimov, Isaac. *Alpha Centauri: The Nearest Star*. New York: Lothrop, Lee and Shepard Co., 1976.

_____. *Words from the Myths*. Boston: Houghton-Mifflin Co., 1969.

Avery, Catherine B., ed. *The New Century Handbook of Greek Mythology and Legend*. New York: Meredith Corp., 1962

Bulfinch, Thomas. *Bulfinch's Mythology*. New York: Avenal Books, 1979.

Cleminshaw, C. H. *Beginner's Guide to the Skies: A Month-by-Month Handbook for Star Gazers and Planet Watchers*. New York: Thomas Y. Crowell Co., 1977.

D'Aulaire, Ingri, and Edgar Parin D'Aulaire. *Book of Greek Myths*. Garden City, New York: Doubleday and Co., Inc., 1962.

Gallant, Roy A. *The Constellations: How They Came to Be*. New York: Four Winds Press, 1979.

Grant, Michael, and John Hazel. *Gods and Mortals in Classical Mythology*. New York: Dorset Press, 1979.

Grant, Michael. *Myths of the Greeks and Romans*. New York: New American Library, 1962.

Graves, Robert. *The Greek Myths*. 2 vols. New York: Viking-Penguin, Inc., 1960.

Hamilton, Edith. *Mythology*. New York: New American Library, 1940.

Rieu, E. V., trans. *Homer: The Odyssey*. New York: Viking-Penguin, Inc., 1946.

Rose, H. J. *A Handbook of Mythology*. New York: Dutton Co., 1959.

Schmidt, Joel. *Larousse Greek and Roman Mythology*. New York: McGraw-Hill, 1980.

Sobol, Donald J. *The Amazons of Greek Mythology*. New York: A. S. Barnes and Co., Inc., 1972.

Tatlock, Jessie M. *Greek and Roman Mythology*. New York: The Century Co., 1917.

Zimmerman, J. E. *Dictionary of Classical Mythology*. New York: Harper and Row, 1964.